W9-AGE-215

CHEFS' CONFIDENTIAL
Secret techniques and signature recipes made kosher

אמונה
EMUNAH

This is a collection of original and adapted recipes.

Published by EMUNAH of America
7 Penn Plaza
New York, N.Y. 10001
(212) 564-9045

ISBN: 978-0-9790824-0-5

A CONSOLIDATED GRAPHICS COMPANY

800.548.2537 wimmerco.com

credits

EDITOR-IN-CHIEF
Michele RB Friedman

ASSISTANT EDITOR
Sherri Herring

PHOTOGRAPHER
John Uher

FOOD STYLIST
Melanie Dubberley

LAYOUT AND DESIGN
Randy Krevat

COMMITTEE CHAIR
Bonnie Eizikovitz

RECIPE TESTING CHAIRS
Aviva Appleman Jacobowitz
Heddy Klein
Fanny Malek
Gladys Neuman
Malkie Spitz

ART REPRESENTATION
Renana Salmon

COPY EDITORS
Syma Shulman Levine
Naomi Rosenblum
Neal Rosenblum
Marlene Walter
Rhonda Weiss

ASSISTANT COPY EDITORS
Natalie Bober
Milton Heumann

BUSINESS MANAGER
Adele Dubin

EVENT PLANNERS
Sharon Brickman Haberman
Esther Lerer

EMUNAH LIAISON
Jani Cooperberg
Rita Goldstone
Annette Goodman
Naomi Leibler
Melanie Oelbaum
Karen Perl
Adele Roffman
Carol Sufian
Reva Tokayer
Leah Weiner

PROFESSIONAL SUPPORT
American Metalcraft
Louise Fisher
Mazur's Marketplace
Stellar Marketing
Thomas Shipley
Yanky Brach of Brach's

donors

Nash Family Foundation

Anonymous in memory of Norma Kligman

MASTER CHEF

Shelli and Harvey Dachs
Bonnie and Jack Eizikovitz
Heddy and Mendy Klein
Cecelia and Rubin Margules

EXECUTIVE CHEF

Sharon and Sinclair Haberman
Fanny and David Malek
The Chaim Foundation

PASTRY CHEF

Maralyn and Isidore Friedman
Judy and Edward Steinberg

SAUCIER

Baslaw, Finger, Friedman, Neuman and Smith Families
Sherry and Neil Cohen
Friedman and Klatt Families
Jeffrey Gejerman
Esther and Paul Lerer
The Avi Yosef Foundation

LINE CHEF

Debbie and Saul Bienenfeld
Faye and Chaim Fortgang
Zahava and Tzvi Goldstein
Sherri and Rabbi Basil Herring
Virginia and Rabbi Robert Hirt
Linda and Rabbi Mark Karasick
Gitta and Jack Nagel
Miriam and Jack Rudman

dedication

This book is dedicated to

HELEN NASH

a leading light in the art of Jewish Cooking. Her commitment to furthering the mission of EMUNAH continues to nourish both bodies and souls.

recipe testers

Robin Abada
Elsa Adler
Abe Alper
Debra Alper
Daniel Asher
Susan Atlas
Robin Baslaw
Yaffa Baslaw
Betty Bendavid
Lee Benjamin
Lou Benjamin
Brynde Berkowitz
Ruthy Bodner
Mehry Cohen
Shelli Dachs
Sara Ezer
Ronnie Faber
Toby Feder
Atara Feinberg
Annette Baslaw-Finger
Shana Finkelstein
Sharon First
Benjamin Friedman
Cheryl Wachtel Friedman
Connie Friedman
Joshua Friedman
Jacob Friedman
Maralyn Friedman
Sarit Friedman
Tali Friedman
Aliza Genauer
Eden Glickman
Miriam Gordon
Andy Grunwald
Linda Grunwald
Cheryl Harris
David Herring
Esti Herring
Yael Herring
Liana Hersh
Rachel Hersh
Bernice Joszef
Randi Kirshenbaum
Terry Kirshenbaum
Robin Klatt
Sam Klatt
Chani Klein
Gaylann Klonsky
Regina Koenig
Sharon Kolb
Hadassah Kotel
Amy Lazar
Millie Leben
Evie Leifer
Megan Leifer
Ahuva Lilker
Sandy Lilker
Danielle Lovett
Jayne Luger
Rachelle Mandelbaum
Elaina Merlis
Malkie Nathan
Ariella Neuman
Cali Orenbuch
Laura Pauli
Karen Perl
Debby Perlman
Aliza Pilevsky
Evelyn Poppick
Ruth Prince
Judy Rosenblatt
Lori Rosner
Esther Schlanger
Betty Shusterman
Bailey Sigman
Jenny Siscovick
Susan Smith
Debbie Steinberg
Judy Steinberg
Naomi Strook
Gaby Taub
Josh Taub
Debbie Teicher
Mimi Thurm
Beverly Walton

emunah mission

Before there was the modern State of Israel, there was EMUNAH. Since 1935, religious Zionists the world over have been expressing their devotion to the rebirth of the Jewish homeland through their work in our organization, first known as Hapoel Hamizrachi, later renamed EMUNAH (faith).

The new name aptly described our dedication to the mission and mandate of our organization, the heart and soul of who we were: we had faith in the vitality and renaissance of the Jewish people and the Jewish homeland. We had faith that, from barren landscapes and infertile fields, cities could rise and a new nation could be born. We had faith that we could co-partner and should co-partner with G-d in making this new Jewish enterprise work. But most importantly, the new name signified our belief in the best of human nature, the potential that resides within every human being. We believed that with the proper education, rehabilitation, social services support and financial aid, we could resurrect individuals and whole families. We believed in this incontestable truth: when you mend an individual, you mend his world. The better one individual functions, the better the society around him functions as well.

We parlayed this belief into creating residential homes for abused and neglected children, giving them the psychological, physical and educational support that make them whole again, making them capable of becoming productive citizens. We actualized this belief by creating educational and social welfare programs for new immigrants, helping to ease and facilitate their successful integration into Israeli society. We augmented this belief by building day care centers and after-school centers for 10,000 children, freeing and enabling their parents to work. We developed this belief through the establishment of an outstanding educational network of vocational schools, high schools and a college of arts and technology. These schools enabled teenagers and young adults from the entire spectrum of Israeli society to acquire skills that make them self-sufficient, economically independent and psychologically whole.

As the country of Israel evolved, matured and changed, so too, did EMUNAH, always adapting to and addressing the current needs of the Jewish State. In addition to EMUNAH's original educational and social welfare institutions located throughout Israel, EMUNAH has added a plethora of new programs that meet the present-day demands of a country that is experiencing both daunting challenges and extraordinary technological advances.

Today, EMUNAH continues to forge ahead, serving as one of Israel's primary backbones and a buttress of support for all its citizens. The proceeds from this cookbook will help us continue to build and rebuild Israel and the Jewish future, one child, one family at a time.

Yitta Halberstam
Co-author *Small Miracles*

Artistic rendition by Renana Salmon, currently a student enrolled at EMUNAH'S Appleman College of Art and Technology.

table of contents

introduction

The "wow!" factor is that special technique, that subtle combination of flavors, that special something that raises your curiosity and makes you ask, "How do they do that?!" Welcome to the exclusive club of international chefs who figuratively stand by your side in your own kitchen and walk you through the steps of preparing each recipe. Then, when the food is finally prepared, they will not abandon you to guess what to do next. They will teach you how to plate and garnish each dish.

Since our aim is to achieve, with ease and economy of time, meals that emulate what the best chefs in finer restaurants create, it helps to understand what happens behind the scenes in restaurant kitchens, known as the "back of the house." First, a chef shops for only the freshest products, develops a recipe and preps the ingredients. Prior to any actual cooking or baking, a chef begins with his mantra mise en place, or "everything in its place." Every ingredient is measured and readied. This step ensures a cooking process that proceeds quickly and efficiently. Equipment on hand includes a chef's knife, a sharpening steel, a sharpening stone, a mandoline (a sharp tool that is used for uniformity in slicing), a cutting board, measuring cups, mixing spoons, squeeze bottles and heavy-weight pots and pans. Easily accessible are shallots, garlic, and fresh herbs. Sounds begin to fill the kitchen: sizzling as meat sears, bubbling as sauce simmers, knocking as knives chop, humming as an immersion blender purees. In no time, enticing aromas join the sounds of the kitchen: onions, garlic, olive oil, wine. Attentively and lovingly, the chef skims the stocks and selects choice herbs.

Sight and smell are the first two senses that lead to our appreciation of food. Plating enriches that first impression and sets the stage for the palate experience. With the utmost of care, the fruits of the chef's labor are strategically placed on the plate. Then come the final touches: the spooning of a sauce, the flick of the wrist as chopped herbs are sprinkled, one final scrutinizing look before the wiping of the plate's rim. All along, the chef's ultimate goal is to obtain the "wow!" factor. The chef's satisfaction comes in that dramatic moment when an artfully arranged plate is set before the diner. With this in mind, our photographs display each prepared recipe on a simple white rimmed plate, making the food, not the tableware, the visual center of attraction.

Remember, the eating experience should be a source of pleasure on a daily basis, not just when entertaining. May this book inspire you to bring your cooking and presentation to a level that will bring delight to your family every day. Once you decide which recipe you would like to prepare, get your mis en place ready, roll up your sleeves, don your chef's toque and apron — it's time to cook like a chef!

On behalf of myself and the assistant editor, Sherri Herring, I wish to express appreciation to: the many chefs who offered their insights, styles and preferences and especially Helen Nash for understanding the importance of this project and for sharing her passion for culinary arts; John Uher and Melanie Dubberley for the stunning photography and creative food styling; Wimmer Printing for walking us through the publishing process step by step; Bonnie Eizikovitz for putting the wheels in motion; Randy Krevat for her artistic eye and flair for style; Debbie Niderberg for demonstrating care and concern; our committee — Adele Dubin, Annette Goodman, Sharon Brickman Haberman, Aviva Appleman Jacobowitz, Heddy Klein, Esther Lerer, Fanny Malek, Gladys Neuman and Malkie Spitz; copy editors — Syma Shulman Levine, Naomi Rosenblum, Neal Rosenblum, Marlene Walter and Rhonda Weiss; Emunah — specifically Naomi Leibler, Melanie Oelbaum, Adele Roffman and Carol Sufian; Sherri's family — Rabbi Basil Herring and children for their unending patience in tasting again and again and again; and to all of our recipe testers and cookbook sponsors.

On a personal note I express appreciation to my children, grandchildren, siblings, my father and step-father, my in-laws — the first people I shared my excitement with after the photo shoot, my mother who walked the pavements of New York City, Paris and Jerusalem with me, begging our way into professional kitchens in order to meet some of the best of the best, my husband, Gary — together we have gone to graduate school, medical school and culinary school, and have most recently edited a cookbook! Finally, and most importantly I express my deepest appreciation to Hashem for allowing me to continue to realize my dreams.

Michele RB Friedman, Editor

the new chef's kitchen

As you begin your partnership with the professional chefs, here are some guidelines for the most efficient and stress-free way to use this book.

1. We suggest you read the entire recipe, including the note, before beginning to do any actual cooking. Often it is helpful to learn how to best purchase, prepare or store an ingredient from the onset.

2. Make a shopping list. Establish a relationship with your butcher, fish monger and other suppliers. They will prove to be invaluable allies.

3. When ready to create a dish, prepare your mis en place. Lay out all the ingredients in the order in which they will be used. This eliminates the possibility of omitting an ingredient. Ready all the utensils which will be required.

THE EFFICIENT KITCHEN

Frequently, kitchen cabinets and drawers are brimming over with gadgets that never get used. This problem is exacerbated in a kosher kitchen where there are doubles (meat and dairy) and sometimes even triples (parve) of equipment. Although not all-inclusive, here is a list of some of the more essential pieces of equipment:

1. *Pots and Pans* — The best material from which pots and pans are made is comprised of three layers. The middle layer, which conducts heat, should be aluminum. Many chefs favor stainless steel for the outer and inner layers. The following pots and pans will be used most frequently: two 10-inch sauté pans, one of which should be high-quality non-stick that does not scratch easily, because, once scratched, the pan needs to be replaced; an 8-inch omelet pan; a grill pan (if you do not have or do not want to use an outdoor grill); three different size pots - all with lids (2-quart sauce pan, 4-quart sauce pan and a stockpot); and a Dutch oven. For baking, assorted baking pans, including both an 8-inch and 9-inch square pan; round cake pans; a Bundt pan; and a jelly roll pan will also prove to be useful.

2. *Knives* — When purchasing a knife, first hold the handle and test it for comfort. Control is determined by hand comfort and the length of the blade. The three most useful knives are likely to be a chef's knife, a paring knife and a serrated knife.

3. *Additional Utensils* — Stainless steel mixing bowls in various sizes; a colander; dry and liquid measuring cups; measuring spoons; wooden spoons; a metal serving spoon; a slotted spoon; a ladle; a variety of spatulas including metal, non-stick, off-set and fish; a whisk; tongs; a vegetable peeler; a microplane zester; a box grater; a ricer or potato masher; a mandoline with a protective glove; poultry shears; kitchen scissors; cutting boards; a meat thermometer; a kitchen timer; a pepper mill; a citrus squeezer; a melon baller; a salad spinner; a pastry brush; ring molds; a pastry bag with assorted tips; and a rolling pin.

4. *Small Appliances* — a food processor; a standing blender; an immersion blender; a standing mixer; and an inexpensive electric coffee mill for grinding spices.

5. *Food Staples* — Kosher salt; fleur de sel; olive, canola and peanut oil; balsamic, red and white wine vinegar; Dijon mustard; ketchup; mayonnaise; breadcrumbs and panko crumbs; tomato paste; vegetable and chicken broth; all purpose flour; granulated and brown sugar; cocoa powder; vanilla extract; assorted spices (whole and ground cumin seed; black peppercorn; ground pepper; turmeric; ground cinnamon; cinnamon sticks; nutmeg; paprika; chili powder; star anise; oregano; and bay leaves).

As you sharpen your skills as a sophisticated chef, you may wish to add items which you personally find helpful.

appetizers

Mousse Filled Basket with
Mixed Greens, Goat Cheese and Mango Salad

Napoleon of Grilled Vegetables

Asian Beef Salad

Seared Duck, Braised Endive
and Puff Pastry Pear

Filled Quince

Mock Crab Cakes

Confit Vidalia Onion, Roasted Tomato
and Goat Cheese Tart

Korean Style Short Ribs

Vegetarian Fire Chili
with Sweet Corn Cakes

Chicken Spring Rolls

Mousse Filled Basket with Mixed Greens, Goat Cheese and Mango Salad

SERVES 8 | PREP TIME: 25 MINUTES | COOK TIME: 8-10 MINUTES

SUN-DRIED TOMATO VINAIGRETTE

- ½ cup extra virgin olive oil
- ¼ cup red wine vinegar
- ¼ cup sun-dried tomatoes packed in oil
- 1 teaspoon minced garlic
- 1 teaspoon salt
- 1 teaspoon ground black pepper

PARMESAN BASKET AND GOAT CHEESE MOUSSE

- 2 cups freshly shredded Parmesan cheese
- 2 ounces soft goat cheese
- 2 tablespoons heavy cream
- 1 teaspoon minced chives
- salt and freshly ground black pepper

SALAD

- ½ head romaine lettuce, coarsely chopped
- ½ head red leaf lettuce, coarsely chopped
- 1 mango, seeded, peeled and ½-inch cubed
- 2 ounces soft goat cheese, cubed
- ½ cup dried cranberries

To make vinaigrette, combine oil, vinegar, tomatoes, garlic, salt and pepper in a food processor. Pulse until tomatoes are finely chopped. Set aside.

For Parmesan basket, heat a griddle or non-stick pan over medium heat. Working quickly, sprinkle ¼ cup Parmesan cheese into a 5-inch circle. Cook until underside is golden brown and top is light gold, about 4 minutes. Watch carefully, if the crisp gets too brown, it will result in a bitter taste. Use a flexible metal spatula to slide under and remove. Drape this over the bottom of an upside down glass; press to form cheese basket. Repeat with remaining cheese until there are a total of 8 crisps.

For mousse, place goat cheese in a food processor. Pour cream through feed tube and continue to process until mixture is smooth. Add chives; mix just to combine. Adjust seasoning with salt and pepper to taste. Place mousse in a piping bag with a medium star tip or into a plastic bag with corner snipped off. Pipe about 1 tablespoon of mousse into each basket.

To make salad, combine romaine and red leaf lettuce, mango, goat cheese and dried cranberries. Toss with enough vinaigrette to coat.

TO PLATE: *Place basket in center of plate, with salad alongside.*

NOTE: *Chef Thomas Keller's Parmesan crisp — the focal point — a lacy textured basket made of only one ingredient, serves as the perfect container for the goat cheese mousse, with a scrumptious salad as its accompaniment. If you are looking for a "wow" type of dish, as only a chef would serve, look no further!*

Only freshly shredded Parmesan cheese can be used for the crisps. Jarred cheese will not melt properly.

Chef Thomas Keller, one of the most inventive American chefs, is as renowned for his well-honed culinary skills as he is for his ability to establish a restaurant that is relaxed and exciting. A chef with exceptionally high standards, Keller's The French Laundry, Bouchon and Per Se have earned him only the highest ratings and many prestigious awards. The filled crisps have been adapted from *The French Laundry Cookbook*.

Napoleon of Grilled Vegetables

SERVES: 4 | PREP TIME: 20 MINUTES | COOK TIME: 35 MINUTES

NAPOLEON

- 1 small to medium eggplant, sliced into ½-inch rounds
- 2 zucchini, sliced into ½-inch rounds
- 2 sprigs rosemary
- 2 sprigs thyme
- ¼ cup extra virgin olive oil
- ¼ cup balsamic vinegar
- 2 teaspoons crushed garlic
- 1 teaspoon kosher salt
- ⅛ teaspoon ground black pepper
- 4 red bell peppers
- 2 red onions, sliced into ½-inch rings
- ½ cup store-bought pesto
- salt

GARNISH

- ¾ cup packed basil leaves plus 4 basil sprigs, divided
- ¾ cup extra virgin olive oil

Variations in colors, architectural creativity and strong grill marks set the stage for a most impressive appetizer. The presentation, however, is just an initiation to something that is equally notable in flavor, provided by Newman and Leventhal Caterers located in New York.

Place sliced eggplant and zucchini in a large sealable plastic bag. Remove leaves from rosemary and thyme. Chop leaves. Add to bag along with oil, vinegar, garlic, salt and pepper. Set aside for a minimum of 15 minutes or overnight. Meanwhile, roast red bell peppers on a hot grill or under the broiler, rotating until skin is black on all sides, about 10-15 minutes. When cool enough to handle, remove charred skin by rubbing with a paper towel. Discard seeds. Cut into 12 square pieces. Set aside. Place eggplant slices on a very hot, preheated and greased grill. After 2 minutes, using tongs, rotate eggplant ¼-turn clockwise so that there are criss-cross grill marks. After 2 minutes, turn over. Remove from grill after 3 minutes. Grill zucchini and onion slices, about 5 minutes per side. Set aside.

Prepare basil oil by placing packed basil leaves into a strainer. Dip strainer into rapidly boiling salted water for exactly 15 seconds. Remove and immediately plunge into ice water. Drain cold herbs and squeeze dry. Chop. Place in blender with oil. Blend for 2 minutes. Pour basil oil into a jar. Put a piece of cheesecloth over jar and pour the oil through the cheesecloth into a squeeze bottle. Discard cheesecloth with purée. To assemble, prepare 4 individual servings. Begin layering vegetables with eggplant, coated thinly with 1 teaspoon pesto, then zucchini, red bell pepper, onion. Repeat eggplant, pesto, zucchini, red bell pepper and top each serving with an eggplant slice that has the best grill marks. Season with salt to taste.

TO PLATE: *Place each napoleon in the center of a small plate. Dot basil oil on one side. Garnish with a basil sprig.*

NOTE: *The only grill markings that really visually matter are the ones on the 4 slices of eggplant that will serve as the top. To clean basil, remove leaves from stems and place leaves in a bowl of cold water. Spin very dry in a salad spinner. Store leaves refrigerated in a sealed plastic bag lined with a paper towel. As long as the leaves are dry they will remain green for several days.*

Asian Beef Salad

SERVES: 6 | PREP TIME: 10 MINUTES PLUS 2 HOURS MARINATING | COOK TIME: 50 MINUTES

BEEF

1½ pounds London broil

MARINADE

¼ cup soy sauce

1½ teaspoons chopped garlic

½ cup pineapple juice

½ teaspoon chopped ginger

freshly ground black pepper

DRESSING

⅛ cup soy sauce

⅛ cup orange juice

2 teaspoons lime juice

1 teaspoon chopped garlic

SALAD

1 medium-size red bell pepper, cut into thin strips

½ pound uncooked snow peas

3 scallions, chopped

1 (10-ounce) package salad greens

OPTIONAL GARNISH

¼ cup peanuts, chopped coarsely

In a sealable plastic bag, place London broil. Add soy sauce, garlic, pineapple juice, ginger and pepper. Seal and refrigerate for at least 2 hours. Preheat oven to 350 degrees. Spray a grill pan with non-stick cooking spray. Heat pan over high heat. Grill London broil for 10 minutes on each side, then place it in oven and continue to cook for 30 minutes. Transfer meat to cutting board and loosely tent foil over the meat. Cool and slice thin on diagonal.

Meanwhile, in a small bowl, whisk soy sauce, orange juice, lime juice and garlic. In a large bowl, dress red bell pepper, snow peas, scallions and salad greens with enough dressing to coat.

TO PLATE: *With tongs, place tossed salad onto individual plates. Fan London broil slices and lean against salad. Spoon dressing on top. Sprinkle with chopped peanuts, if desired.*

NOTE: *In a professional kitchen, when time is of the essence, ginger is peeled with the back of a spoon or a peeler. It can then be chopped with a chef's knife or in a food processor and stored refrigerated, covered with white vinegar in a sealed container. This same technique can easily be incorporated into a home kitchen. When ready for use, squeeze out vinegar and measure amount needed. The vinegar does not impart a strong flavor to the ginger and its acidity will retard the possibility of the ginger spoiling.*

No dinner party at the Cabot House at Harvard University in Cambridge, Massachusetts, would be complete without the grilled Asian-style London broil salad made by Dick Nickinson of Sweet Berry Café & Catering. The combination of tender, perfectly flavored meat with a crunchy salad is sure to be received with as much enthusiasm at your table as it is by Harvard's faculty and students.

Seared Duck, Braised Endive and Puff Pastry Pear

SERVES: 4 | PREP TIME: 20 MINUTES | COOK TIME: 1 HOUR

DUCK OR CHICKEN

1 tablespoon Hoisin sauce
1 tablespoon Dijon mustard
1 tablespoon ketchup
2 tablespoons grape jelly
4 (4 to 6-ounce) duck breasts or chicken thighs, with skin, de-boned
freshly ground black pepper
½ tablespoon Chinese five spice powder
1 tablespoon canola oil

Preheat oven to 375 degrees. In a small bowl, combine Hoisin sauce, mustard, ketchup and jelly. If using duck, trim away excess fat and, with a sharp knife, cut a criss-cross pattern into the skin without penetrating meat. Place a sauté pan over moderate-high heat. Season duck or chicken with black pepper on flesh side only and Chinese five spice powder on skin only. Add oil to pan. Just prior to smoking, add poultry to oil, skin-side down, and cook for 5 minutes, allowing skin to brown. Reduce heat to low; turn over and cook an additional 5 minutes. Discard fat in pan. Flip over again and brush crisp skin with Hoisin mixture. Put into oven for 7 minutes. Cut into slices.

PEAR IN PUFF PASTRY

4 seckel pears, washed and thoroughly dried
½ (17.3-ounce) package puff pastry sheets (1 sheet)
2 teaspoons chopped walnuts
1 egg yolk mixed with 2 teaspoons water
1 teaspoon cinnamon sugar

To prepare each pear, while being careful to keep stem intact, turn pear over in your hand so that the base is facing upwards. With melon baller, scoop out seeds from base. Turn pear right-side up and place on a parchment-lined jelly roll pan. Bake for 13 minutes. Let cool.

Lightly roll out puff pastry sheet on a floured surface into a 12-inch square. Cut into 4 (6-inch) squares. Hold pear upside down in your hand. Place ½ teaspoon chopped nuts in hollowed out portion of each pear. Flip over in the palm of your hand and lay pastry square on top of stem, punching a hole in dough with stem point. Pull corners down and around pear, pressing seams gently to enclose pear with nuts inside. Brush bottom with egg yolk mixture to seal. Place pear standing up, sealed-side down onto parchment-lined jelly roll pan. Brush with egg yolk mixture. Sprinkle with cinnamon sugar. Bake until golden brown, about 25-30 minutes.

Joey Bodner, Marty Bodner and Eddie Izso of Main Event Caterers, based in Englewood, New Jersey, always receive rave reviews. Their motto "we don't just cater, we cater to you" could not be more true.

BELGIAN ENDIVE

2 tablespoons canola oil
1 shallot, chopped
1 leek, white portion only, small dice
4 heads endive
salt and freshly ground black pepper
1 small sprig thyme
1½ cups chicken broth
½ teaspoon sugar

In a small sauté pan, heat oil. Add shallots and leeks. Sauté until soft, about 4 minutes. Place endive on top of shallots and leeks. Season with salt and pepper; add thyme, chicken broth and sugar. Cover and bring to a boil; reduce heat and simmer 20 minutes. Slice endive into very thin long pieces. These thin, ribbon like slices are referred to as chiffonade.

GARNISH

4 sprigs flat-leaf parsley

TO PLATE: *Place bed of endive chiffonade in middle of plate. Fan sliced duck or chicken on top with pear to upper left. Add parsley as garnish.*

NOTE: *Currently, home cooks can only obtain kosher duck breasts by purchasing the entire duck. This recipe can therefore be prepared by using the duck breasts and the remaining thighs can then be made into confit (a technique in which duck is salted and then cooked under its own fat). Unlike chicken, duck breast should be medium-rare and still pink in the center. If cooked well-done, it will be dry and tasteless. Another option is to substitute chicken thighs for duck breasts. Although not as exotic, the chicken will also result in a truly memorable dish.*

Chinese five spice powder can be purchased in the spice section of your supermarket. It incorporates the five basic flavors of Chinese cuisine — sweet, sour, bitter, savory and salty, and is composed of cinnamon, fennel, star anise, cloves and pepper.

Filled Quince

SERVES: 6 | PREP TIME: 15 MINUTES | COOK TIME: 2½ HOURS

6 medium-size quinces
½ cup brown sugar, divided
1 onion, thinly sliced
½ pound ground chicken or turkey
¼ cup rice
½ cup water
1 teaspoon salt
¼ teaspoon ground black pepper
1 teaspoon cinnamon
½ teaspoon cardamom
½ teaspoon cumin
1 cup apple juice
2 tablespoons extra virgin olive oil
¼ cup balsamic vinegar
¼ cup lime juice
¼ teaspoon saffron, dissolved in 1 tablespoon hot water

Introducing individuals to the pleasures of Persian cuisine has been a lifelong mission for Najmieh Batmanglij. She is an award-winning author. Her repertoire includes: *Ma Cusisine d'Iran, New Food of Life — Ancient Persian and Modern Iranian Cooking and Ceremonies, Persian Cooking for a Healthy Kitchen* (source of this recipe, Mage 1994), *A Taste of Persia: An Introduction to Persian Cooking* and *Silk Road Cooking: A Vegetarian Journey*. She has spent the past 26 years traveling, teaching and adapting authentic Persian recipes to tastes and techniques of the West.

Wash and rub quinces to remove fuzz. Cut off a disk ¼-inch thick from the top of each fruit which serves as the lid; set aside. Using a knife tip or melon baller, scoop out and reserve pulp, leaving a ½-inch thick outer edge; discard seeds. Sprinkle 1 teaspoon brown sugar in each quince shell. In a large non-stick skillet, sauté onion and ground chicken or turkey over medium heat for 15 minutes; add rice, water, salt, pepper, cinnamon, cardamom and cumin. Bring to a boil; reduce heat, cover and simmer 15 minutes. Fill each quince with rice stuffing. Replace tops and arrange side by side in a deep, lidded pan. Add apple juice and quince pulp to pan and pour 1 teaspoon oil over each quince. Using an adapted Persian cooking technique, place 2 layers of paper towel over pan and cover tightly with lid. Simmer 1 hour. In a saucepan, combine vinegar, lime juice, remaining brown sugar and saffron water; lift up paper towel and pour liquid mixture over quince. Replace paper towel and cover. Cook 45-60 minutes, basting occasionally with pan juices.

TO PLATE: *Place one quince on each dish. Prop lid pointing upwards. Surround with pan juices.*

NOTE: *The quince, an incredibly tart seasonal fruit in the apple and pear family, combines flavors of guava, pineapple, apple and Bartlett pear, but cannot be eaten raw. However, when cooked, its spicy tartness, paired with chicken or beef, creates a perfect balance. When purchasing, select a large firm fruit without blemishes. Store at room temperature until peel turns from green to yellow, but fruit is still firm. During other times of the year, when quince becomes unavailable, feel free to substitute a baking apple.*

Saffron, with its vivid red-orange color, delicate bittersweet flavor and honey-like fragrance, is a spice that comes from the stamen of flowers, primarily grown in Iran, Spain and India. It takes about 4,330 flowers to produce one ounce of saffron. The threads can only be harvested by hand, hence it is the world's most expensive spice. However, most recipes require a very small amount of this exotic ingredient, usually a half-teaspoon or less. Saffron is sold as threads or powder. The powder may have additives, like turmeric, so it is best to buy the threads.

Mock Crab Cakes

SERVES: 8 | PREP TIME: 20 MINUTES PLUS 2 HOURS (OR OVERNIGHT) REFRIGERATION | COOK TIME: 25 MINUTES

CRAB CAKES

- ½ cup vegetable oil, divided
- 3 tablespoons mayonnaise
- 1½ tablespoons lime juice
- 1 teaspoon prepared white horseradish
- ¾ teaspoon salt
- ½ teaspoon ground black pepper
- 1 (16-ounce) package imitation crabmeat, flaked into small pieces
- ¼ red onion, small dice
- 1 scallion, green part only, thinly sliced
- ¼ red bell pepper, small dice
- 1 tablespoon chopped cilantro
- ½ cup breadcrumbs
- ¼ cup all purpose flour
- 1 egg
- 1½ cups panko or cornflake crumbs

LIME-CHILI SAUCE

- ½ cup chili sauce
- 1 lime, juiced
- 1 tablespoon toasted sesame oil

There is one restaurant in particular that is known for its crab cakes. We were unable to obtain their recipe, but brought many to our test kitchen. Relentless with our experimentation, we are now confident that we were able to unlock the secret to this great recipe.

Line a jelly roll pan with parchment paper; set aside. In a bowl, whisk ¼ cup oil, mayonnaise, lime juice, horseradish, salt and pepper. Fold imitation crabmeat, onion, scallion, red bell pepper, cilantro and breadcrumbs into mixture. Shape crab cakes by squeezing out any liquid and firmly forming 16 patties. Place on prepared jelly roll pan; cover with plastic wrap and refrigerate 2 hours.

To prepare sauce and relish, in a small bowl, use a spoon to mix chili sauce, lime juice and sesame oil. Set aside. In another bowl, combine mango, red bell pepper, cucumber, jalapeño, lime juice and sesame oil. Refrigerate until needed.

To cook cakes, preheat oven to 425 degrees. Place flour into a dish. In a separate bowl, whisk egg. On another plate, place panko crumbs. Dredge crab cakes first in flour on all sides, then in egg, then panko crumbs. Pour remaining ¼ cup oil into a baking dish large enough to hold a single layer of cakes. Heat pan with oil in oven for 5 minutes. Carefully remove baking dish and place cakes into pan. Return to oven and bake until golden brown, about 10-12 minutes on each side. For garnish, whisk lime juice and sesame oil in a small bowl, then lightly dress mesclun greens. Season with salt and pepper to taste.

TO PLATE: *Prop 1 crab cake against another on an appetizer plate. Spoon 2 tablespoons of mango relish onto crab cake that is lying flat on plate. Drizzle or spoon lime-chili sauce alongside crab cakes and garnish plate with dressed greens.*

MANGO RELISH

½ cup peeled and ¼-inch diced mango
½ red bell pepper, ¼-inch dice
½ cup peeled and ¼-inch diced seedless cucumber
½ small jalapeño pepper, seeded and ⅛-inch dice
1 lime, juiced
1 teaspoon toasted sesame oil

GARNISH

1 lime, juiced
1 tablespoon toasted sesame oil
1 cup mesclun or assorted baby greens
salt and freshly ground black pepper

NOTE: *In a restaurant kitchen, there are many times when large quantities of food need to be sautéed. When burners are limited and time is of the essence, one way around this is to blast the oven with very high heat. Oil is added to a jelly roll pan and heated, followed by the food item. In our case, we wanted to avoid deep frying and therefore utilized this technique.*

Panko, also known as Japanese breadcrumbs, is noted for its crunchy, lighter texture and is often preferred by chefs as a breading, over standard breadcrumbs.

Confit Vidalia Onion, Roasted Tomato and Goat Cheese Tart

SERVES: 6 | PREP TIME: 1 HOUR PLUS 30 MINUTES REFRIGERATION | COOK TIME: 1½ HOURS

EQUIPMENT NECESSARY

6 (4 x 1-inch) removable bottom tart pans

TART DOUGH

¾ cup unsalted butter at room temperature
2½ teaspoons sugar
1½ teaspoons salt
2 tablespoons milk
1 large egg
2 cups all purpose flour

TART FILLING

5 plum tomatoes
¼ teaspoon salt
⅛ teaspoon ground black pepper
2 tablespoons extra virgin olive oil
1 teaspoon chopped dried thyme
¼ cup heavy cream
¼ cup milk
¼ teaspoon salt
⅛ teaspoon cayenne pepper
1 egg
2 teaspoons extra virgin olive oil
2 Vidalia onions (about 1½ pounds), thinly sliced
¾ (4.4-ounce) package goat cheese

GARNISH

6 thyme sprigs

Preheat oven to 350 degrees. To prepare dough, in a mixer or food processor, beat butter, sugar and salt until creamy. Add milk and egg; mix until smooth. Add flour and mix just until dough is formed. Form into a ball, cover with plastic wrap and refrigerate 30 minutes.

Slice tomatoes into ¼-inch slices. Toss in bowl with salt, pepper, oil and thyme. Arrange on a jelly roll pan in a single layer and roast in oven until tender, about 20 minutes. Set aside. With mixer, beat cream, milk, salt, pepper and egg until smooth. Set aside. Place oil in a large sauté pan over low heat and sauté onions, stirring periodically until completely tender and light brown, about 25 minutes. Remove dough from refrigerator and divide into 6 round balls. With a rolling pin, roll dough between 2 pieces of lightly floured parchment paper into flat discs ¼-inch thick. Fit into tart pans, rolling the pin over the top to cut off excess dough. Butter 6 small squares of aluminum foil and fit them, butter-side down, into each of the tart pans. Fill the foil with uncooked rice or beans. Place the tarts onto a jelly roll pan. Bake 20 minutes. Remove beans and foil from tart shell, prick bottom all over with a fork, and bake an additional 5 minutes. Remove tart shells from oven. Fill tarts halfway with sautéed onions. Spoon 2½ tablespoons of batter into each shell. Bake until set, about 15 minutes. Remove from oven and arrange 5 slices roasted tomato on top, overlapping in a circle. Top with 1 tablespoon goat cheese. Put back in oven for 7 minutes, or until tart is firm when shaken and top is lightly browned. Remove tart from pan.

TO PLATE: *Place hot tart on plate. Lay thyme sprig alongside.*

NOTE: *Select firm, bright and "tomato-smelling" tomatoes. Store them at room temperature to ripen. Never refrigerate tomatoes, as the refrigeration destroys both the flavor and texture. Use a serrated knife to slice tomatoes in order to maintain their shape.*

Blind-baking refers to a process of baking a pie or tart crust without the filling. The crust is lined with foil or parchment paper, and then filled with uncooked rice or beans, so that it will keep its shape when baking. After the crust is baked, the rice or beans are replaced with the filling. Blind-baking prevents the crust from becoming too soggy and allows the crust to bake longer than the filling. Save the beans or rice in a designated container for the next time you bake tarts.

Judy Marlow, founder and owner of Simply Divine, an upscale kosher catering company in New York City, is one of the most sought-after party planners. Judy recognized talent when she named Brian Sutor, formerly sous chef to Georges Perrier at Le Bec Fin in Philadelphia, her executive chef. Together, Judy and Chef Brian know how to prepare and present food that is befitting their name... simply divine!

Korean Style Short Ribs

SERVES: 8-10 | PREP TIME: 10 MINUTES PLUS OVERNIGHT MARINATING | COOK TIME: 8 MINUTES

RIBS

4 pounds short ribs or flanken

MARINADE

1 cup soy sauce

1 cup ponzu sauce

1 cup mirin

½ cup rice vinegar

½ cup toasted sesame oil

½ cup sake, vermouth or dry white wine

1 cup dark brown sugar

¼ cup lemon juice

½ cup prepared tehina

2 tablespoons chili sauce

2 scallions, chopped

2 tablespoons minced garlic

2 tablespoons chopped ginger

GARNISH

2 cups cooked jasmine rice

2 scallions, green part only, cut into 2-inch pieces, then thinly sliced lengthwise into ¼-inch strips

½ cup chopped chives

Place ribs into a container. In a large bowl, combine soy sauce, ponzu sauce, mirin, vinegar, oil, sake, sugar, lemon juice, tehina, chili sauce, scallions, garlic and ginger; pour over ribs and cover. Refrigerate overnight.

Take ribs out of refrigerator; bring to room temperature. Prepare jasmine rice according to directions on package. Heat grill. Remove ribs from marinade and grill 4 minutes; turn over and grill an additional 4 minutes for medium-rare.

TO PLATE: *Serve 2 short ribs per person on a bed of jasmine rice. Slice the tip of one scallion strip into a Y-shape. Rest a second strip onto the Y-tip of the first. Place these two scallion strips like a teepee on top of the short rib. Sprinkle outer edge of plate with chives.*

NOTE: *Ponzu sauce, a citrus based condiment, strongly tart in flavor, is used in Japanese cuisine. It is comprised of soy sauce, lemon or lime juice and rice vinegar. If you cannot find ponzu sauce, use an additional ½ cup lemon juice.*

Dark sesame oil is made from toasted or roasted sesame seeds. This thick, rich oil is golden to dark brown in color and is very aromatic. Because of its low smoke point (the temperature at which the oil smokes or burns), it is used as an assertive, distinctive flavoring agent, as opposed to being used as an oil for frying. It should be stored in a cool place, away from light.

There are some people that just do not want to share their secret recipe. Gabriel Abikzer, Executive Chef of Genadeen Caterers on Long Island, New York, while attending a neighbor's barbeque, refused to accept a no share policy. So he tasted carefully, closed his eyes, mentally recorded his rendition, ran home, put on his apron and created his own secret amazing Korean Style Short Ribs. Here it is!

Vegetarian Fire Chili with Sweet Corn Cakes

SERVES: 9 | PREP TIME: 20 MINUTES | COOK TIME: 1 HOUR

CHILI

- **1 tablespoon canola oil**
- **½ yellow onion, ¼-inch dice**
- **¼ red bell pepper, ¼-inch dice**
- **¼ yellow bell pepper, ¼-inch dice**
- **¼ jalapeño pepper, minced**
- **1 clove garlic, minced**
- **½ teaspoon ground chipotle pepper (increase for more heat)**
- **¾ teaspoon ground cumin**
- **½ teaspoon onion powder**
- **½ teaspoon garlic powder**
- **½ teaspoon dried oregano**
- **1 (14-ounce) can diced tomatoes with juice**
- **¼ cup frozen whole kernel corn**
- **½ (15-ounce) can kidney beans, drained**
- **1½ teaspoons honey**
- **salt**

In a heavy-bottom stockpot, heat oil over medium-high heat. Add onion, red and yellow bell peppers, jalapeño pepper and garlic. Cook for 10 minutes. Add chipotle pepper, cumin, onion and garlic powders and oregano. Stir 2 minutes. Add tomatoes. Reduce heat to low and simmer until thickened, about 15 minutes. Stir in corn and kidney beans. Simmer 10 minutes. Add honey. Season to taste with salt.

SWEET CORN CAKES

- **1 (10-ounce) package frozen whole kernel corn, thawed**
- **½ cup butter or margarine, softened**
- **⅓ cup masa harina (if not available, substitute yellow cornmeal)**
- **¼ cup water**
- **2 tablespoons heavy cream**
- **⅓ cup sugar**
- **¼ cup yellow cornmeal**
- **½ teaspoon baking powder**
- **¼ teaspoon salt**

Preheat oven to 350 degrees. Process corn in a food processor, pulsing until coarsely chopped. In the bowl of an electric mixer, beat butter or margarine until creamy. Gradually beat in masa harina or cornmeal. On low speed, beat in water. Add cream. Add chopped corn. In a separate bowl, combine sugar, cornmeal, baking powder and salt. Stir into corn mixture. Pour into an ungreased 8-inch square pan and cover with foil. Place in larger baking dish and pour boiling water halfway up sides of outer pan, creating a water bath to prevent burning. Bake 50-60 minutes or until set. Remove pan from water. Uncover and let stand 15 minutes. Cut into 9 squares.

GUACAMOLE

2 ripe avocados, peeled and pitted
2 tablespoons fresh lime juice
2 tablespoons chopped fresh cilantro
2 teaspoons seeded and minced jalapeño pepper
salt
canola oil

In a medium bowl, coarsely chop avocados with a fork. Add lime juice, cilantro and jalapeño, keeping the coarse texture. Season to taste with salt. Drizzle top with oil. Press plastic wrap directly on surface of guacamole. Refrigerate to allow flavors to develop.

GARNISH

½ cup sour cream
¼ cup shredded Cheddar cheese
¼ cup minced scallions, green part only
¼ cup minced red onion

TO PLATE: *Place corn cake in center of a plate. Top with a heaping spoonful of chili, a spoonful of guacamole, a dollop of sour cream and a sprinkle of Cheddar cheese. Garnish with scallions and onions.*

NOTE: *Although not a staple item in many homes, masa harina or corn flour, is available in many larger grocery stores. If you have the opportunity to purchase masa harina, it is worthwhile for this recipe. When combined with cornmeal, sugar, butter and cream, a delightful pudding-cake is created.*

Melanie Dubberley, our amazingly talented food stylist, was the inspiration for this recipe. With an undergraduate degree in Food Biochemistry and Studio Art, Melanie furthered her education at the Culinary Institute of America. With over 15 years experience in the food industry, Melanie specializes in food styling and has appeared in *Chocolatier* and *Pastry Art & Design* magazines. In addition to food styling, she expertly develops and tests recipes and writes culinary articles.

Chicken Spring Rolls

YIELD: 26 ROLLS | PREP TIME: 30 MINUTES PLUS OVERNIGHT MARINATING | COOK TIME: 20 MINUTES

CHICKEN AND MARINADE

1½ tablespoons brown sugar
1 tablespoon salt
4 cloves garlic, chopped
1½ tablespoons dry sherry
2 teaspoons soy sauce
1 tablespoon cornstarch
¾ pound boneless chicken breasts cut into matchstick strips
1 tablespoon peanut oil

VEGETABLES AND WRAPPERS

1 cup assorted mushrooms: button, baby Portobello, crimini and shiitake, caps only, thinly sliced
1 medium head napa cabbage, finely shredded
½ carrot, shredded
2 scallions, thinly sliced
2½ teaspoons soy sauce
1 teaspoon salt
1 teaspoon sugar
1 (1-pound) package egg roll wrappers
1 egg, beaten
4 cups peanut oil for frying, or as needed

DIPPING SAUCE

1 cup apricot preserves
2 teaspoons red horseradish
2 teaspoons Teriyaki sauce

In a small bowl, combine brown sugar, salt, garlic, sherry, soy sauce and cornstarch; add chicken. Cover and refrigerate overnight. Heat oil in a wok or large skillet over high heat. Add marinated chicken and cook 4-5 minutes. Add mushrooms, cabbage, carrot, scallions, soy sauce, salt and sugar; cook 2 minutes.

To assemble, place wrapper on a work surface in a diamond shape with one corner pointing towards you. Place 3 tablespoons of filling onto bottom third of wrapper. Brush egg on edges of wrapper. Fold bottom corner over filling and roll. Fold left and right sides over egg roll and continue rolling tightly. Lay seam-side down; cover with plastic wrap. In a deep fryer or a pot, heat oil until hot, but not smoking (350 degrees). Fry rolls, 4 at a time, until golden brown. Avoid overcrowding the pan as this reduces the oil temperature. Drain egg rolls on paper towel.

Prepare dipping sauce in small bowl by stirring together apricot preserves, horseradish and Teriyaki sauce.

TO PLATE: *Cut spring rolls in half. Serve with sauce.*

NOTE: *In China, crispy egg rolls, fried golden brown, are served to usher in the Chinese New Year marking the start of spring; hence, they are also known as spring rolls.*

Peanut oil is to Asian cuisine as olive oil is to Mediterranean cooking. Peanut oil is appreciated for its high smoke point, which means that it can be heated to a high temperature without burning and is therefore desirable in frying foods. Frying, due to the high temperature of the oil, enables food to be cooked quickly from the outside in. The result is a crispy, golden brown exterior, with a tender, moist inside. If the oil is not hot enough, the food being fried will absorb the oil, resulting in food that is soggy, greasy and undesirable. If the oil is too hot, the food will brown quickly, but the inside will not be cooked. To determine the correct temperature of the oil, use a thermometer, or look for the formation of tiny little bubbles when the food is added to the oil.

Although spring rolls at Le Carne Grill in New York City are traditionally made with beef in a ranch sauce, Chef Angel Ramirez's adaptation, combined with our own, will have your guests licking their fingers, savoring every morsel.

soups

Refreshing Chilled Strawberry Soup

French Onion Soup with Baguette Croutons

Parsnip and Fennel Soup

Vegetable Soup En Croûte

Roasted Tomato Soup with Fresh Basil

Baghdadi Red Lentil Soup

Roasted Garlic Potato Soup

Butternut Squash Apple Soup
with Candied Pumpkin Seeds

Pat's Famous Minestrone Soup

Creamy Carrot Ginger Bisque

Flanken Mushroom Barley Soup

Creamy Cauliflower Soup with Crispy Shallots

Chilled Gazpacho with Melon

Refreshing Chilled Strawberry Soup

SERVES: 4-6 | PREP TIME: 10 MINUTES | COOK TIME: NONE

4 pints strawberries, hulled, reserve 6 small strawberries for garnish
1 mango, peeled, pitted and halved
1 peach, peeled, pitted and quartered
1 (20-ounce) can crushed pineapple
1 cup orange juice
6 tablespoons sugar
6 mint sprigs for garnish

In a food processor, purée strawberries, mango, peach, pineapple, orange juice and sugar in 2 batches. When smooth, combine batches in a large container. Cover and refrigerate until ready to serve. For garnish, place a strawberry, stem-side down, on a cutting board and cut slits almost to the stem; do not cut entirely through the strawberry. Gently fan out the slits, accordion-style. Stick a mint sprig where stem would be.

TO PLATE: *Pour soup into a bowl or martini glass and top with strawberry mint garnish.*

NOTE: *The biggest strawberries are not always the best tasting. By selecting brightly colored, smaller but still plump berries, you will find that the flavor is more concentrated. Store unwashed strawberries in an airtight container in the refrigerator.*

When strawberries take center stage at the peak of their season, chefs utilize them in the most creative manner. Using an assortment of fruits packed with vitamin C, this refreshing soup, with its thick frothy texture and fruity flavor, is a most welcomed dish.

French Onion Soup with Baguette Croutons

SERVES: 8 | PREP TIME: 10 MINUTES | COOK TIME: 2½ HOURS

- **2 tablespoons butter**
- **2 tablespoons olive oil**
- **8 large yellow onions, thinly sliced**
- **1 teaspoon salt plus extra to taste**
- **1½ teaspoons all purpose flour**
- **2 quarts parve beef or parve chicken flavored broth**
- **½ cup brandy, or ¼ cup port wine with ¼ cup balsamic vinegar**
- **1 bouquet garni: 4 sprigs thyme (plus extra for garnish), 4 sprigs flat-leaf parsley, 1 bay leaf, wrapped in cheesecloth and tied with kitchen twine**
- **freshly ground black pepper**
- **8 (½-inch thick) baguette or French bread slices**
- **olive oil**
- **12 ounces grated Swiss or mozzarella cheese**

Chef Anthony Bourdain, chef and author, once said that traveling to other countries helped him to reconnect with what is enduringly great about French food. Onion soup is right up there. Chef Bourdain's work served as the inspiration for this soup.

To prepare broth, in a large heavy stockpot, melt butter with oil over medium heat. Add onions and 1 teaspoon salt. Reduce heat to low. Stir onions every 15 minutes until they are soft and brown, about 1½ hours. Do not allow them to blacken. Add flour; cook over medium-high heat, stirring for 2 minutes. Add broth, brandy or port wine with vinegar. Add bouquet garni to soup. Reduce heat and simmer for 1 hour. Remove bouquet garni. Season to taste with salt and pepper.

To prepare croutons, preheat broiler. Place bread slices on a jelly roll pan. Brush both sides with oil and sprinkle lightly with salt. Place under broiler and toast; turn and brown other side. Watch carefully as bread will burn quickly. Leave broiler on; remove toast and set aside. Ladle hot soup to within ½-inch of top of oven-safe bowls. Sprinkle heaping amount of cheese on top of crouton. Float crouton on top of soup and place bowls under broiler until cheese melts, bubbles and browns.

TO PLATE: *Place bowl on napkin-lined plate. Sprinkle thyme on top of soup.*

NOTE: *Onions are easier to slice if you leave the root intact after you cut them in half. Cooking onions very slowly ensures that natural sugars will caramelize, rather than just browning the surface through sautéing. This process should take a long time; it requires a watchful eye and intermittent stirring. This is really the key to the soup's success. After that, it is about the ratio of the four primary building blocks: the fullness of the broth, the sweetness of the onions, the soaked through croutons and the molten, stringy, crispy, crusted cheese. If you do not have oven-safe bowls, toast cheese over the croutons on a jelly roll pan, and float them as a garnish on the soup.*

To get rid of onion or garlic odor on your hands, rub your hands on anything that is stainless steel — a bowl, the sink or a pot — under cold running water. The odor dissipates.

Parsnip and Fennel Soup

SERVES: 10-12 | PREP TIME: 25 MINUTES | COOK TIME: 45 MINUTES

- **2 tablespoons plus ½ cup vegetable oil, divided**
- **3 pounds (approximately 8) large parsnips, diced, plus 1 for garnish**
- **1 yellow onion, diced**
- **1 leek, white part only, chopped**
- **2 fennel bulbs, sliced, reserve fronds for garnish**
- **1 stalk celery, chopped**
- **1 tablespoon salt**
- **¾ teaspoon ground black pepper**
- **¼ cup white wine**
- **1½ quarts vegetable broth or parve chicken broth, plus more as needed**
- **½ cup heavy cream or soymilk, plus ¼ cup for garnish**
- **salt and freshly ground black pepper**

Heat 2 tablespoons oil in large stockpot. Add parsnips, onion, leek, fennel, celery, salt and pepper. Sauté until softened, approximately 8 minutes, stirring occasionally. Add wine and cook on medium-high heat until liquid is evaporated, about 3 minutes. Add broth. Simmer 30 minutes. Using an immersion blender, purée until smooth. Pour in ½ cup cream. Blend again until combined. Add additional broth until desired consistency is obtained. Soup should be thick and creamy. Season with salt and pepper to taste. For garnish, peel remaining parsnip with a vegetable peeler. Heat a sauté pan with ½ cup oil. When hot, add parsnip strips and fry until golden. Remove and place on paper towel to drain. Season with salt to taste.

TO PLATE: *Pour remaining ¼ cup cream into a squeeze bottle. Ladle soup into a bowl. Garnish with fried parsnip, reserved fennel fronds and a decoration of cream.*

NOTE: *Fennel, also called sweet anise, with its intimidating odd shape, is often bypassed by shoppers in the produce section because of confusion with mislabeling it as anise, a pungent herb. Fennel's strength is in its power to blend and enhance flavors. When cooked, the fennel softens and becomes sweeter, like an onion, retaining only a faint hint of anise. As for parsnip, when it is slowly sweated (sautéed) until tender, it imparts a sweet earthy flavor. Together, they create a soup that is unidentifiable, but scrumptious. To prepare the fennel, begin by cutting off both the bottom root and the top stalks where they meet the "bulb" (actually not a bulb at all, but tightly stacked leaves, like the base of a celery stalk). Reserve the fronds, fragrant emerald sprigs that resemble dill, for the garnish. Use a mandoline or a sharp knife to thinly slice the bulb.*

Many great recipes are born in the kitchens of adventurous, talented home chefs who are willing to experiment, taste and revise. Through this experimentation, flavors that otherwise might not be intertwined, merge — bringing out the best in each other.

Vegetable Soup En Croûte

SERVES: 6 | PREP TIME: 25 MINUTES | COOK TIME: 45 MINUTES

- 6 tablespoons olive oil, divided
- 3 tablespoons water
- 2 small leeks, white part only, ¼-inch dice
- 2 small potatoes, peeled, ¼-inch dice
- 1 small onion, ¼-inch dice
- 2 stalks celery, ¼-inch dice
- 1 medium zucchini, ¼-inch dice
- 12 green beans, ¼-inch dice
- 2 medium carrots, peeled, ¼-inch dice
- 2 quarts chicken broth
- 3 ripe plum tomatoes, peeled and seeded
- 28 fresh basil leaves, washed and dried, 18 of these reserved for top
- 4 medium garlic cloves
- salt and freshly ground black pepper
- 1½ (17.3-ounce) packages puff pastry sheets (3 sheets)
- 1 egg yolk
- 1 tablespoon water

In a stockpot, combine 3 tablespoons oil with water. Add leeks, potatoes, onion, celery, zucchini, green beans and carrots; sauté over medium-low heat about 6 minutes; avoid browning vegetables. Add broth and bring to a boil. Simmer 30 minutes. Meanwhile, in a food processor, purée tomatoes, 10 basil leaves, garlic and remaining 3 tablespoons oil. Stir purée into cooked soup. Do not let soup return to a boil. Season to taste with salt and pepper. Allow to cool.

Preheat oven to 400 degrees. To create bowl covers, place 1 sheet puff pastry on floured parchment paper. Cut dough into 2 circles, the same size as the top of the 13-ounce oven-safe bowls that will be used for serving. Place clusters of 3 individual basil leaves in the center of each circle. Place another piece of parchment paper on top of dough. Roll until the circle is ½ inch bigger all around when compared to the top of bowl. Repeat until there are 6 covers. Whisk egg yolk and water together. Ladle soup three-fourths full into 6 serving bowls. With a pastry brush, moisten upper outside edge of bowls with egg wash. Cover bowl with herbed pastry. With your fingers, press the dough onto the bowl to seal. Poke a sharp knife in a few locations evenly around top to vent. Brush with egg wash. Bake until golden brown, about 15-20 minutes.

TO PLATE: *Place bowl on napkin-lined plate.*

NOTE: *En Croûte is a French term referring to a food that is baked encased in a pastry crust.*

Austrian born Wolfgang Puck began his formal culinary training at the age of fourteen. He honed his skills in France and later in the United States. He is the star attraction at many restaurants including Ma Maison and Spago and is the author of several cookbooks. During the course of his illustrious career, Chef Puck has received accolades including a James Beard Award for Outstanding Chef of the Year. This soup was inspired by a recipe created by the Chef.

Roasted Tomato Soup with Fresh Basil

SERVES: 8 | PREP TIME: 10 MINUTES | COOK TIME: 1 HOUR 5 MINUTES

SOUP

4½ pounds ripe plum tomatoes, halved lengthwise
6 cloves garlic, minced
4 Vidalia onions, quartered
¼ cup olive oil
1 teaspoon kosher salt
1 quart vegetable broth
2 tablespoons tomato paste
1 teaspoon sugar
1 cup fresh basil leaves, thinly sliced
salt and freshly ground black pepper

GARNISH

8 basil sprigs
8 breadsticks

Preheat oven to 400 degrees. On a baking sheet toss tomatoes with garlic, onions, olive oil and salt. Arrange in a single layer; roast 45 minutes until edges of tomatoes begin to blacken. Scrape everything from pan into stockpot; add broth, tomato paste and sugar. Simmer for 20 minutes. With an immersion blender, purée soup. Season to taste with salt and pepper.

TO PLATE: *Serve soup in mugs garnished with basil and accompanied by breadsticks.*

NOTE: *This is the best tomato soup ever! Truth be told, sumptuous home grown tomatoes are hard to ruin. This recipe puts the spotlight on the appeal of bright colors and vibrant fresh taste that are the gifts of the summer season. Plum tomatoes, also known as Roma and Italian, are a favorite for both soup and sauce, since this variety is fleshier and has fewer seeds. When slow roasted in the oven, the sweet vine ripened flavor is more intensified.*

The best way to store tomato paste is to measure out tablespoons into a mini ice cube tray. Once frozen, pop cubes out into sealable plastic bags and store in the freezer for later use.

Vidalia onions are an unusually sweet variety of onion, due to the low amount of sulfur in the soil in which they are grown. Aside from their sweetness, they cause less eye irritation when chopping.

Chef Carole Sobell of England, caterer par excellence and author of the fabulous *New Jewish Cuisine* (Kuperard), continues to amaze us with her exquisite recipes. This soup was adapted from one in her repertoire.

Baghdadi Red Lentil Soup

SERVES: 6-8 | PREP TIME: 15 MINUTES | COOK TIME: 1 HOUR 35 MINUTES

- **1 pound red lentils**
- **¼ cup olive oil**
- **3 large onions, chopped**
- **1 tablespoon finely chopped garlic**
- **1 tablespoon finely chopped ginger**
- **2 teaspoons cumin**
- **1 teaspoon turmeric**
- **2 tablespoons salt**
- **½ tablespoon ground black pepper**
- **4 bay leaves**
- **2 plum tomatoes, diced**
- **1 red hot chili pepper (optional)**
- **3 quarts water**
- **⅓ cup fresh lemon juice**
- **2 lemons, sliced for garnish**
- **8 cilantro sprigs**

Wash lentils and check carefully for stones. Wash again until water runs clear. Heat oil in a heavy stockpot over medium-high heat. Add onions, stirring gently. After 5 minutes, add garlic, ginger, cumin and turmeric. Stir until well mixed. Add lentils and stir until they are well coated with spices. Add salt, pepper, bay leaves, tomatoes and chili, if using. Add water and bring to a boil. Reduce heat and simmer, covered, for about 90 minutes, stirring regularly. If water is absorbed, add more as needed. Remove bay leaves. Using an immersion blender, purée soup. Add lemon juice and more water if consistency is too thick.

TO PLATE: *Ladle soup into bowl. Top with lemon slices and cilantro sprig.*

NOTE: *Lentils, named for their lens shape, should be stored in a sealed container at room temperature. They should be rinsed and picked over to remove any small stones. However, they do not require presoaking as their small, thin size allows for quick cooking.*

The proper method of cleaning fresh herbs is to put them into cold water. Drain and replace with fresh water; repeat until water is clear of dirt and any other undesirables. Dry herbs in a salad spinner, or in a towel. To store, wrap them in a paper towel placed in a sealed plastic bag and refrigerate.

Chef Hila Solomon has created a boutique, private dining experience where guests enjoy a culinary adventure in her historic home located in Yemin Moshe, Jerusalem's first neighborhood outside the walls. Excellence in cuisine, service and atmosphere in the house, garden and terrace, with breathtaking panoramic views, have gained Spoons an international reputation for being comparable to the finest restaurants anywhere in the world. Hila offers private anthropological and culinary tours of the Mahane Yehuda shuk, and wine and cheese tours around Israel.

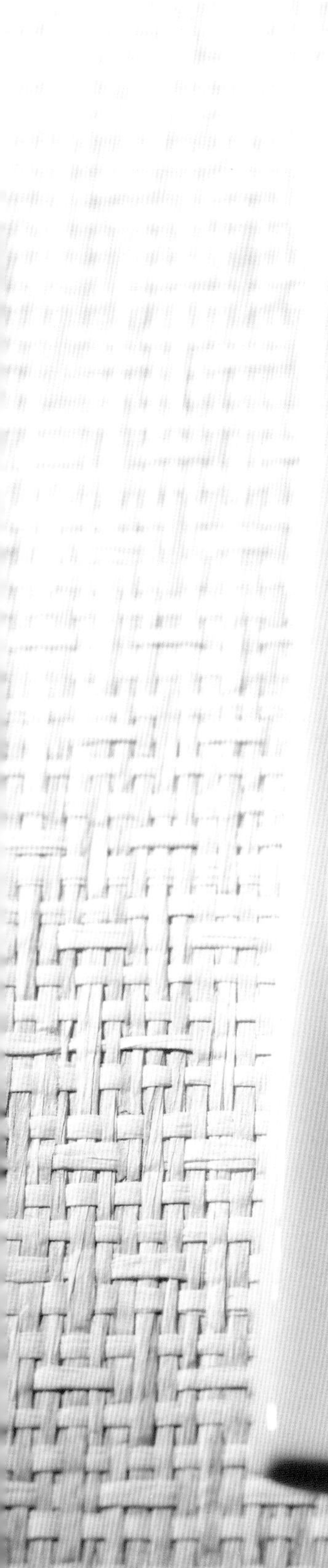

Roasted Garlic Potato Soup

SERVES: 8-10 | PREP TIME: 15 MINUTES | COOK TIME: 2 HOURS

- **5 garlic heads, unpeeled**
- **5 tablespoons olive oil, divided**
- **1 pound Spanish onions, ¼-inch dice**
- **2 stalks celery, ¼-inch dice**
- **1 carrot, ¼-inch dice**
- **2 quarts vegetable or chicken broth**
- **1 bouquet garni: 4 sprigs parsley, 4 sprigs thyme, 1 bay leaf, wrapped in cheesecloth and tied with kitchen twine**
- **1½ pounds Idaho potatoes, peeled and ½-inch dice**
- **1 teaspoon salt**
- **⅛ teaspoon ground black pepper**

Preheat oven to 350 degrees. Cut off top ¼-inch of garlic heads. Drizzle 3 tablespoons oil over garlic heads and place in a small shallow baking dish. Bake 1 hour. Cool slightly. Using your fingers, press individual cloves from 4 garlic heads, squeezing out garlic into a bowl. Reserve cloves from 1 head for garnish. Set aside.

In a 5-quart heavy bottom stockpot, sauté onions in remaining 2 tablespoons oil. Cook until just beginning to brown, about 5 minutes. Add celery, carrot, garlic, broth and bouquet garni; bring to a boil. Add potatoes, reduce heat and simmer 1 hour. Remove bouquet garni and purée 2 cups of soup in a blender. Return puréed soup to pot; stir in salt and pepper. Taste and adjust seasoning with salt and pepper.

TO PLATE: *Ladle soup into warmed bowls. Garnish with reserved garlic cloves.*

NOTE: *When purchasing garlic, avoid heads with small green sprouts. Store in a cool, dry place. Roasting mellows the flavor of garlic and softens it into a paste.*

In a professional kitchen, rather than using cheesecloth, a bouquet garni is often wrapped in the green portion of a leek. The leek is then folded and tied with kitchen twine to resemble a parcel package.

Regardless of the time of day, anyone who shops in Toddy's, owned by Jay Todtman, on Long Island, New York, must be prepared to brave the crowds. Known for many specialties, if you arrive at Toddy's midday, this soup is guaranteed to be sold out.

Butternut Squash Apple Soup with Candied Pumpkin Seeds

SERVES: 6 | PREP TIME: 10 MINUTES | COOK TIME: 50 MINUTES

SOUP

- **¼ cup canola oil**
- **4 yellow onions, chopped**
- **1 tablespoon curry powder**
- **5 cups chicken or vegetable broth, divided**
- **2 butternut squash (3 pounds total weight), peeled and chopped**
- **4 Fuji apples, peeled, cored and diced**
- **2 teaspoons salt**
- **½ teaspoon ground black pepper**

PUMPKIN SEEDS

- **1 teaspoon margarine**
- **½ cup raw pumpkin seeds**
- **1 tablespoon sugar**
- **pinch paprika**
- **pinch cayenne pepper**
- **kosher salt**
- **1 teaspoon honey**

APPLE SAGE GARNISH

- **1 tablespoon canola oil**
- **1 red Macintosh apple, seeded, thinly sliced (⅛-inch)**
- **3 sage leaves, thinly sliced**

Heat oil in a stockpot. Add onions and curry powder. Cook covered over low heat until onions are softened, about 20 minutes. Add 4 cups broth, squash and apples. Bring to a boil. Reduce heat and simmer, partially covered, for 25 minutes. With an immersion blender, purée soup, adding as much of remaining 1 cup broth as needed for desired creamy consistency. Season with salt and pepper.

For pumpkin seeds, melt margarine in a small pan. Add pumpkin seeds, sugar, paprika, cayenne pepper and salt. Toss to coat. Cook just until they color slightly, about 1½ minutes. Turn off heat. After 30 seconds add honey.

Spread seeds on a plate and allow to cool.

For apple garnish, heat oil in a skillet over low heat. Add apple slices in a single layer. Cook for 1 minute or until apple slices soften, but are not brown.

TO PLATE: *Ladle soup into a bowl. Arrange 2-3 slices of apples in a cluster floating on top of the soup. Sprinkle soup with pumpkin seeds and sage leaves.*

NOTE: *Toasted pumpkin seeds also make a great garnish on a tossed salad.*

Respected chefs will make frequent trips to outdoor markets before planning their menu for the day. Prior to making any purchase, however, the first step taken is to survey the area. While at the Union Square Greenmarket in New York, one producer explained the importance of respecting the food and the individuals who grow it. Deep in conversation, butternut squash and sage came into focus which is classically combined in a variety of cuisines. The introduction of Fuji apples was suggested by the producer, making the perfect creamy blend of these autumn treasures.

Pat's Famous Minestrone Soup

SERVES: 8-10 | PREP TIME: 20 MINUTES PLUS OVERNIGHT REFRIGERATION | COOK TIME: 1 HOUR 15 MINUTES

2 medium yellow onions, ¼-inch dice
¼ cup olive oil
2 carrots, ¼-inch dice
2 stalks celery, ¼-inch dice
5 cloves garlic, minced
1 teaspoon dried oregano
½ cup chopped flat-leaf parsley
10 fresh basil leaves, cut into thin strips, reserve a sprinkling for garnish
1 (28-ounce) can diced tomatoes
2 zucchini, ¼-inch dice
2 medium russet potatoes, ¼-inch dice
1 (16-ounce) can white beans, undrained
2 quarts chicken or vegetable broth
salt and freshly ground black pepper

Sauté onions in oil over medium heat in a large stockpot until translucent, about 5 minutes. Add carrots, celery, and garlic. Sauté vegetables over moderate heat until they are half cooked, about 10 minutes. Add oregano, parsley, basil, tomatoes, zucchini, potatoes, undrained beans, broth, salt and pepper. Bring soup to a simmer and cook until all the vegetables are tender, about 1 hour. Allow to cool and refrigerate overnight. Heat prior to serving.

TO PLATE: *Ladle soup into bowl and sprinkle with reserved basil.*

NOTE: *This soup is best served the day after it is prepared so that flavors can develop.*

To cut the basil leaves into thin strips you can either use kitchen scissors or you can stack the leaves, roll them, and then cut them with a chef's knife into thin strips. Chefs refer to this technique as chiffonade.

Pat Fine, originally from Johannesburg, South Africa, is the owner of Pat's Restaurant and the Master Chef of Pat's Catering in Los Angeles, California. Pat has been, and remains, a kosher cuisine pioneer in Los Angeles and was dubbed by Rabbi Meyer May of the Simon Wiesenthal Center, the "queen of kosher catering, absolutely top of the line."

Creamy Carrot Ginger Bisque

SERVES: 8-10 | PREP TIME: 20 MINUTES | COOK TIME: 1 HOUR 15 MINUTES

½ cup olive oil
1 Vidalia onion, sliced
1 fennel bulb, sliced
2 pounds carrots, sliced
1 pound parsnips, peeled and sliced
1 tablespoon salt, divided
1 bay leaf
8 sprigs fresh thyme (4 using leaves only, 4 for garnish)
1 (1-inch) piece fresh ginger, peeled and sliced
2 quarts plus 1 cup water, divided
1 tablespoon honey
freshly ground black pepper
black sesame seeds and toasted pumpkin seeds for garnish

Preheat a large stockpot over medium-high heat. Add oil, onion and fennel; sauté covered for 15 minutes or until softened, stirring every 5 minutes. Add carrots and parsnips. Add 2 teaspoons salt. Cover pot and reduce heat to medium-low. Cook 30 minutes. Add bay leaf, thyme leaves and ginger. Add 2 quarts water. Simmer 30 minutes. Remove from heat. Remove and discard bay leaf. Add honey and remaining 1 teaspoon salt. Using an immersion blender, purée soup. Add as much of the remaining 1 cup water as needed for desired consistency. Taste and adjust seasoning with salt and pepper.

TO PLATE: *Serve soup hot, with a sprinkling of sesame and pumpkin seeds and a sprig of thyme for garnish.*

NOTE: *When storing carrots, chop off and discard the top greens, as they rob moisture from the carrot.*

Chef Michael Gershkovich was born in Rome, Italy. A graduate of the Culinary Institute of America, Chef Mike worked in California and Hawaii before opening Mike's Bistro in New York City, a showcase for his cuisine. Visiting this restaurant is like going to Mike's house for a very special meal.

Flanken Mushroom Barley Soup

SERVES: 8 | PREP TIME: 15 MINUTES | COOK TIME: 2 HOURS

- **1 pound flanken**
- **salt and freshly ground black pepper**
- **1 tablespoon canola oil**
- **1 pound onions, ¼-inch dice**
- **10 ounces white mushrooms, sliced**
- **10 ounces shiitake mushrooms, stems removed, sliced**
- **2 teaspoons chopped garlic**
- **⅓ cup pearl barley, rinsed**
- **3 sprigs fresh thyme, leaves only**
- **1½ quarts beef or chicken broth**
- **1 bay leaf**
- **3 tablespoons chopped flat-leaf parsley, divided**

Season flanken with salt and pepper. Heat oil in large stockpot over high heat until hot. Add flanken and allow to become golden brown; turn and brown second side. With tongs, remove flanken and set aside. Reduce heat to medium-high, add onions and sauté until slightly golden brown, about 8 minutes. Add mushrooms. Sauté 2-3 minutes. Add garlic, barley and thyme. Sauté additional 2-3 minutes. Add broth. Scrape bottom of pot, as this is where much of the flavor is captured. Add flanken back to pot along with bay leaf and 2 tablespoons parsley. Cook on moderate heat and bring to a boil. Lower heat to a simmer for approximately 1½ hours. Remove flanken. Cut meat off bone and cut into small pieces. Discard bones. Add meat back into soup. Simmer 15 minutes. Adjust salt and pepper to taste. Discard bay leaf.

TO PLATE: *Ladle into warm bowls and garnish with remaining 1 tablespoon parsley.*

NOTE: *Avoid mushrooms that are blemished or look dried out. Store them refrigerated in a paper bag to maintain humidity.*

If making the soup in advance, adjust the consistency with additional broth when reheating.

The best way to handle a chef's knife is to hold the item to be cut with your fingertips tucked under and your thumb behind them. The blade rests and slides directly against the middle section of your fingers. The guiding fingers move backwards, determining the thickness of the slices.

From the time he was seventeen, Chef David Cooper knew his future was in the kitchen. This dream led him to the Culinary Institute of America where David graduated with honors and distinction. He has been with Prestige Caterers, under the direction of Joel and Spencer Katz for the past seven years, where his flair for originality and creativity has flourished. Prestige Caterers opened its doors thirty-five years ago and has evolved into one of New York's premier kosher caterers.

Creamy Cauliflower Soup with Crispy Shallots

SERVES: 4-6 | PREP TIME: 10 MINUTES | COOK TIME: 30 MINUTES

2 tablespoons margarine

1 onion, chopped

2 carrots, cut into chunks

1 (1½-pound) head fresh cauliflower, cut into chunks, or frozen

4 cups vegetable or parve chicken flavored broth

1½ cups milk

1 teaspoon salt, plus more to taste

¼ teaspoon ground black pepper

GARNISH

2 tablespoons olive oil

½ cup thinly sliced shallots

4-6 sage sprigs

salt

Melt margarine in a stockpot. Add onion and sauté until translucent, about 10 minutes. Add carrots, cauliflower and broth. Simmer until vegetables are tender, about 20 minutes. Using an immersion blender, purée until thick and creamy. Add milk, salt and pepper.

While soup is cooking, prepare garnish, using a non-stick skillet. Heat oil; add shallots and cook 5-10 minutes or until brown and crispy. Add sage and cook for 5 seconds. Remove shallots and sage from pan and place on paper towel to absorb oil. Sprinkle with salt to taste.

TO PLATE: *Ladle into a bowl; garnish with crispy shallots and fried sage.*

NOTE: *The shallot and sage garnish can be made ahead of time and stored in a sealable bag, but do not refrigerate.*

An alternate garnish is shelled pumpkin seeds prepared on a jelly roll pan with a drop of oil, a sprinkle of salt and baked at 350 degrees for 10 minutes.

While attending The French Culinary Institute, culinary students are given the opportunity to work in a variety of professional kitchens. Students encounter one of the more unusual and unique experiences in the kitchen of the Calhoun School in New York City, under the direction of Chef Bobo. The Calhoun lunch service strives to focus on fresh, nutritious, balanced ingredients, while still maintaining a viable school budget. The outcome is almost miraculous as the palates of children are being altered, teaching them to make healthier food choices. This adapted version of Chef Bobo's recipe, demonstrates just how easy it is to get children to eat cauliflower.

Chilled Gazpacho with Melon

SERVES: 8-10 | PREP TIME: 20 MINUTES PLUS 40 MINUTES TO CHILL | COOK TIME: NONE

- **8 plum tomatoes, ¼-inch dice**
- **2 seedless cucumbers, ¼-inch dice**
- **3 red bell peppers, ¼-inch dice**
- **2 red onions, ¼-inch dice**
- **1 small jalapeño pepper, seeded and minced**
- **4 teaspoons minced garlic**
- **¼ cup chopped cilantro**
- **6 cups tomato juice**
- **½ cup white wine vinegar**
- **¼ cup extra virgin olive oil**
- **2 teaspoons salt**
- **1½ teaspoons ground black pepper**

GARNISH

- **½ small ripe honeydew melon, seeded**
- **1 seedless cucumber**

In a bowl, combine tomatoes, diced cucumbers, red bell peppers, onions, jalapeño pepper, garlic, cilantro, tomato juice, vinegar, oil, salt and pepper. Chill soup until cold, 30-40 minutes. Taste and adjust seasoning.

For garnish, using a small melon baller, scoop melon and cucumber balls.

TO PLATE: *Ladle soup into bowls. Garnish with melon and cucumber balls.*

NOTE: *The heat of jalapeño peppers is mostly stored in the seeds and veins. To make them milder, wearing rubber gloves, remove the seeds. Avoid touching your eyes or mouth, as the oils left behind on the gloves can burn.*

Seedless cucumbers, also known as hothouse or English cucumbers, are the long thin ones. Not only is their lack of seeds advantageous, but they tend to be much sweeter than traditional cucumbers.

The best way to select ripe honeydew is just to smell it. It should have a sweet aroma.

The ease and refreshing flavor of one of Spain's most celebrated specialties, gazpacho is most welcome in the heat of the summer. Few soups with its base of tomatoes, peppers, cucumbers, onions and garlic are as easy to make. The melon and cucumber garnish, accentuating the freshness of the soup, takes its inspiration from Asia and is brought to us through the genius of Chef Jean-Georges Vongerichten.

salads

Pear, Curried Cashews
and Dried Cranberry Salad

Roasted Beet Salad with Fried Chickpeas,
Olives and Crumbled Feta

Fennel and Orange Salad

Sushi-Roll Rice Salad

Asparagus, Shiitake Mushrooms, Red Potatoes
and Roasted Chicken Salad

Dijon Salmon, Red Potato
and String Bean Salad

Asian Coleslaw

Black Bean and Quinoa Salad

Crunchy Chicken with Mixed Salad
and Date Dressing

Roasted Portobello Mushrooms
and Baby Arugula Salad

Pear, Curried Cashews and Dried Cranberry Salad

SERVES: 4-6 | PREP TIME: 15 MINUTES | COOK TIME: 20 MINUTES

PEARS AND CASHEWS

3 tablespoons brown sugar, divided

2 ripe, but firm Bosc pears, quartered lengthwise, seeded

1 tablespoon margarine, melted

1 teaspoon chopped fresh rosemary

1 teaspoon curry powder

⅛ teaspoon cayenne pepper

¾ cup roasted cashews

DRESSING

3 tablespoons white wine vinegar

3 tablespoons Dijon mustard

2 tablespoons honey

3 tablespoons extra virgin olive oil

salt and freshly ground black pepper

SALAD

1 (10-ounce) package mixed salad greens

½ cup dried cranberries

Preheat oven to 425 degrees. Place 2 tablespoons brown sugar on a plate. Dip each side of pear into brown sugar, then arrange pears in a single layer on parchment-lined jelly roll pan. Roast 20 minutes. In a bowl, stir together margarine, rosemary, curry powder, cayenne pepper, remaining 1 tablespoon brown sugar and roasted cashews. Set aside.

For the dressing, in a small bowl, whisk vinegar, mustard, honey and oil. Season to taste with salt and pepper. Just before serving, lightly toss greens and pears with enough dressing to coat.

TO PLATE: *Mound greens with pears in center of salad plate. Arrange cashews and dried cranberries on top.*

NOTE: *To prepare the salad greens early, wash and spin dry in a salad spinner; store refrigerated in a sealed plastic bag, lined with a paper towel. The curried cashews and roasted pears can be prepared beforehand as well.*

For a chef, often the inspiration behind a new recipe is based upon ingredients that are in season. This salad, with its rustic colors, is a synthesis of several different ideas, and clearly welcomes the autumn months.

Roasted Beet Salad with Fried Chickpeas, Olives and Crumbled Feta

SERVES: 6-8 | PREP TIME: 30 MINUTES | COOK TIME: 50 MINUTES

3 bunches beets, mixed colors if possible
¾ cup extra virgin olive oil, divided
1½ teaspoons salt, divided
1½ teaspoons cumin seeds
2 tablespoons plus 2 teaspoons red wine vinegar
1 tablespoon lemon juice, plus more for seasoning
1 cup cooked chickpeas, drained
¼ cup thinly sliced shallots
½ cup cured black olives, pitted
½ cup flat-leaf parsley leaves
¼ pound feta cheese
salt and freshly ground black pepper

Preheat oven to 400 degrees. Cut greens off beets and toss with 2 tablespoons oil and 1 teaspoon salt. Place beets in a roasting pan with a splash of water in the bottom. Cover pan tightly with foil and roast until tender when pierced, about 50 minutes. Roasting time will vary depending on size and beet variety, so check them earlier. When done, carefully remove foil. Let cool and, with rubber gloves covering your hands to prevent staining, peel beets by slipping off skins. Slice beets into wedges and place in a large bowl. If beets are small, just cut them in half. While beets are roasting, toast cumin seeds in a medium pan over medium heat 2-3 minutes, until seeds release their aroma and darken slightly. Pound half of cumin seeds to a fine powder in a mortar (or use a clean coffee grinder). Transfer powder to a bowl with remaining cumin seeds, ¼ teaspoon salt, vinegar and 1 tablespoon lemon juice. Whisk in ½ cup oil. Taste for balance and seasoning. Add remaining 2 tablespoons oil to the same pan and heat 2 minutes, until oil is very hot. Add chickpeas and fry 4-5 minutes, shaking pan often, until chickpeas are crispy. Be careful while frying as chickpeas pop and oil can splatter. Drain on paper towels, and season with a few pinches of salt and some pepper. Add shallots to beets, season with ¼ teaspoon salt and a twist of black pepper; gently toss with three-quarters of vinaigrette. Add more lemon juice, salt and black pepper to taste. Gently toss in olives and parsley leaves. Add more vinaigrette if necessary.

TO PLATE: *Place beet salad on individual salad plates. Crumble cheese over and around beets and scatter chickpeas on top.*

Suzanne Goin, an award-winning chef, was born in Los Angeles to food-obsessed, French-loving parents. By the time she graduated with honors from Brown University, she had worked at Ma Maison, L'Orangerie, Al Forno and Le Mazarin. From there, Suzanne worked at Alice Water's Chez Panisse in Berkeley and at Todd English's Olives in Boston. Chef Suzanne opened Lucques in California. Shortly after, she was named by *Food and Wine* magazine as Best New Chef. Then Chef Suzanne opened A.O.C. and, later with her husband, The Hungry Cat. She is the author of *Sunday Suppers at Lucques* which won a James Beard Award. Her focus on taste and the beauty of the plate is reflected in this recipe.

Fennel and Orange Salad

SERVES: 4-6 | PREP TIME: 15 MINUTES | COOK TIME: 12 MINUTES

ORANGE VINAIGRETTE

¼ teaspoon grated orange zest

1 orange, juiced

1 shallot, minced

1 tablespoon apple cider vinegar

1 teaspoon balsamic vinegar

½ teaspoon salt

½ cup extra virgin olive oil

SALAD

1 cup slivered almonds

1 fennel bulb, reserve fronds (feathery leaves like dill) for garnish

1 teaspoon parsley, finely chopped

3 oranges, peeled, and cut into thin rounds

2 large bunches watercress

18 pitted Niçoise olives

Preheat oven to 350 degrees. Prepare vinaigrette by whisking orange zest, juice, shallot, apple cider vinegar, balsamic vinegar, salt and oil. Set aside.

Place almonds on a jelly roll pan. Toast 12 minutes, tossing every 3-4 minutes. Slice bottom off fennel bulb; remove tough outer leaves and discard. Quarter bulb, cut out and discard core; very thinly slice bulb with a mandoline or a knife. Toss with 2 tablespoons of vinaigrette and parsley. Set aside. Place orange slices in a bowl with 2 tablespoons of vinaigrette. Pick small branches off large center stems of watercress and discard any yellow leaves. Wash, dry and set selected watercress aside. When ready to plate, dress watercress with remaining vinaigrette.

TO PLATE: *Layer watercress loosely with oranges, fennel, almonds and olives. Garnish with fronds.*

NOTE: *Wild fennel is commonplace in Sicily. The fronds are intensely anise-flavored, making a beautiful garnish, while the bulbs are crunchy and add a perfect complement to the oranges. If you have never tried fennel, it is also worthwhile braising (simmering in a covered pan) as a side dish. Its flavor changes dramatically.*

I can still remember exactly where I was the first time I tasted this salad. With pen in hand, I took notes and could not wait to get home to recreate it. The salad tastes great, looks pretty and is quite unique.

Sushi-Roll Rice Salad

SERVES: 8 | PREP TIME: 15 MINUTES PLUS SEVERAL HOURS REFRIGERATION | COOK TIME: 20 MINUTES

GARNISH

- 2 scallions
- 8 small red chili peppers
- 1 sheet toasted nori, cut into very thin strips with a pair of scissors, ¼ for garnish, ¾ for salad
- 4 avocados
- 2 lemons, quartered

RICE AND DRESSING

- 1½ cups short-grain sushi rice
- ¼ cup rice vinegar
- 1½ tablespoons toasted sesame oil
- 1 tablespoon soy sauce
- 1 tablespoon sugar
- ½ teaspoon chopped garlic
- ½ teaspoon chopped ginger
- 1¼ teaspoons wasabi paste

SALAD

- 1 carrot, grated
- ½ seedless cucumber, peeled, ¼-inch dice
- ½ red bell pepper, ¼-inch dice
- 3 tablespoons drained, coarsely chopped Japanese pickled ginger
- 1 tablespoon toasted sesame seeds
- 2 scallions, thinly sliced on diagonal

For garnish, with a sharp knife, cut green part of scallions lengthwise into thin strips and place in a bowl of ice water.

For chili flower, using small scissors or paring knife, cut chili lengthwise to form triangular petals, taking care not to cut all the way to stem. Wearing rubber gloves, rinse peppers in cold water; pick out and discard seeds. Add to ice water; refrigerate several hours or overnight.

Cook sushi rice according to directions on package. In the meantime, in a small saucepan, over a low flame, stir vinegar, oil, soy sauce, sugar, garlic, ginger and wasabi paste until sugar is dissolved. Gently add dressing to warm rice. Toss with carrot, cucumber, red bell pepper, ginger, sesame seeds, sliced scallions and three-fourths of nori strips.

Immediately before serving, halve and pit avocado. Lay avocado pitted-side down and gently peel skin, being careful not to gouge avocado flesh. With a sharp knife, slice avocado lengthwise into 1/16-inch slices. Squeeze the juice of ¼ lemon on the sliced avocado half. Using your left hand, place your fingers on the left side of the avocado and thumb on the right side. Move your four fingers in one direction and your thumb in the opposite direction so that the slices gently slide apart vertically. Use your right thumb to help your left thumb with this sliding motion. Add enough lemon juice to help lubricate the avocado so that it slides easily. Then, gently shape avocado vertical slices into an "s" shape. The end pieces of the avocado will not be used.

TO PLATE: *Set a ring form or a small can (with the top and bottom removed) onto an individual plate. Spoon the rice salad into the mold. Using the back of the spoon, pack the rice down into the mold. Lift mold up to remove. With a small offset spatula lift avocado s-shaped slices onto plate, alongside sushi rice. Remove and drain scallion curls. Sprinkle sushi rice with reserved nori and scallion curls. Garnish plate with 1 chili flower.*

NOTE: *There are two main varieties of avocados. Haas, with a dark, thick, leathery skin, is considered to be more desirable than the smooth-skinned Fuerate. Choose firm avocados which yield to pressure. Avocados can be ripened at home in a brown paper bag. Avoid purchasing rock-hard ones that have been picked too early; they will rot before they ripen.*

Sushi, as a culinary experience, is both traditional in ingredients and design, and at the same time ever-changing, a blend of old Japanese culture and innovations of new. Here, ingredients are left intact, yet the concept has been altered — a tactic often incorporated by a chef. Even though the sushi has been reinvented as a salad, the plating and garnish retains the integrity that is most appreciated in the art of sushi presentation.

Asparagus, Shiitake Mushrooms, Red Potatoes and Roasted Chicken Salad

SERVES: 8-10 | PREP TIME: 25 MINUTES | COOK TIME: 20 MINUTES

SALAD

- **¾ pound fresh asparagus, cut into 3-inch pieces**
- **8 ounces shiitake mushrooms, stems discarded, caps thinly sliced**
- **2 garlic cloves, minced**
- **4 tablespoons olive oil, divided**
- **¾ pound small red potatoes, thinly sliced**
- **1 medium-size red onion, thinly sliced**
- **12 ounces mesculin greens**
- **1 pound roasted chicken or duck breast, sliced**
- **3 scallions, thinly sliced**
- **¼ cup pomegranate seeds or sliced strawberries**
- **2 tablespoons toasted sesame seeds**

DRESSING

- **½ cup toasted sesame oil**
- **½ cup soy sauce**
- **2 tablespoons rice wine vinegar**
- **2 tablespoons honey**
- **1 teaspoon minced ginger**
- **1 teaspoon minced garlic**

Preheat oven to 375 degrees. Place asparagus, mushrooms and garlic tossed with 2 tablespoons oil on a jelly roll pan; roast until tender, about 15 minutes. Combine potatoes with remaining 2 tablespoons oil; place in a single layer on another jelly roll pan. Bake until tender, about 20 minutes.

To prepare dressing, in a small bowl, whisk oil, soy sauce, vinegar, honey, ginger and garlic. In a large serving bowl, combine asparagus, mushrooms, potatoes, onion and greens. Add enough dressing to coat.

TO PLATE: *Arrange dressed salad on plate. Overlap chicken or duck slices alongside. Sprinkle with scallions, pomegranate seeds or strawberries and sesame seeds. Drizzle dressing on top.*

NOTE: *The chef originally prepared this dish with duck. However, since it is impossible for the home cook to purchase kosher duck breast exclusively, we have adapted this recipe and are using the breast from freshly purchased rotisserie chicken. The result is definitely not your typical chicken salad!*

The stems of most varieties of mushrooms are edible. The exception is the shiitake stem, which should be removed and discarded. The cap, with its woody flavor that intensifies when cooked, can be cleaned with a damp paper towel. Avoid washing or chopping mushrooms until ready for use. To store, keep in refrigerator away from aromatic items, because they absorb odors like a sponge.

Dijon Salmon, Red Potato and String Bean Salad

SERVES: 6-8 | PREP TIME: 30 MINUTES, PLUS 2 HOURS MARINATING | COOK TIME: 10 MINUTES

SALAD

1 pound skinless salmon fillet

½ cup vegetable or parve chicken broth

1 pound baby red potatoes, quartered

1 pound string beans, cut into 2-inch pieces

2 tablespoons chopped fresh dill, plus sprigs for garnish

DRESSING

1 teaspoon grated lemon zest

⅓ cup fresh lemon juice

2 tablespoons capers

2 tablespoons Dijon mustard

1 teaspoon sugar

½ teaspoon salt

¼ teaspoon ground black pepper

¼ cup extra virgin olive oil

This salad was rescued from piles of treasured recipes. Whoever tastes it, requests it...you be the judge.

Preheat oven to 400 degrees. Place fish into a glass baking dish. Pour broth around salmon. Cover with foil and bake 10 minutes or until salmon is medium-rare. Checking with a knife, separate between flakes, ensuring that center is still slightly translucent. When cool to touch, flake salmon into chunks. Meanwhile, to a medium pot of boiling, salted water, add potatoes. Cook until a knife inserted comes out easily, about 7 minutes. Drain. Add string beans to a pot of boiling salted water; cook 3 minutes. Drain and plunge into ice cold water; drain again.

In a small bowl, combine lemon zest, juice, capers, mustard, sugar, salt, pepper and oil. Two hours before serving, put salmon, potatoes, string beans and dill in a large bowl. Pour dressing over and toss gently.

TO PLATE: *Serve in a decorative dish garnished with dill.*

NOTE: *Knowing when fish should be removed from a heat source is a skill that chefs understand well. Since fish continues to cook for an additional 5 minutes after it is removed from heat, it is important that the fish be slightly undercooked when you remove it. Otherwise the fish will be dry. A general rule of thumb is to cook the fish for 2 minutes less than the estimated time, then check for doneness by separating the flakes with a knife. Both salmon and tuna are better on the rare side, when the center is translucent as opposed to opaque.*

Capers, sun-dried flower buds, are pungent flavor enhancers. Often they are used as a seasoning or a garnishing.

Regardless of the dressing you are preparing, a bit of mustard acts as an emulsifier, a substance that enables the oil and vinegar to mix, preventing them from separating.

Asian Coleslaw

SERVES: 8-10 | PREP TIME: 10 MINUTES PLUS OVERNIGHT MARINATING | COOK TIME: NONE

- **½ cup mayonnaise**
- **2 tablespoons mirin**
- **2 tablespoons rice vinegar**
- **1 tablespoon white vinegar**
- **1 tablespoon soy sauce**
- **1 tablespoon lime juice**
- **2 tablespoons sesame oil**
- **1 (16-ounce) package shredded white or green cabbage**
- **1 (10-ounce) package shredded red cabbage**
- **1 cup chives, cut 2-inches long**
- **½ red onion, thinly sliced**
- **4 scallions, thinly sliced, reserve a sprinkling for garnish**
- **1 jalapeño pepper, seeded and minced**
- **½ cup chopped cilantro, reserve a sprinkling for garnish**
- **salt**
- **white and/or black sesame seeds for garnish**

In a small bowl, whisk mayonnaise, mirin, rice vinegar, white vinegar, soy sauce, lime juice and oil. In a large bowl, combine cabbages, chives, onion, scallions, jalapeño pepper and cilantro. Pour dressing over vegetables. Cover and marinate overnight in the refrigerator. Adjust salt to taste.

TO PLATE: *Serve in an Asian style bowl garnished with reserved scallions, cilantro and a sprinkling of sesame seeds.*

NOTE: *Mirin, an essential condiment in Japanese cuisine, is a rice wine similar to sake, but with a lower alcohol content.*

Rice vinegar is made from fermented rice and is widely used in Asian cooking. With a hint of sweetness, which comes from the glutinous rice, it is less acidic and milder in flavor than Western vinegars.

A chef is always tasting and adjusting. Here, salt is gingerly added after marinating the coleslaw to enhance the flavor.

When a chef eats something in a restaurant that he or she loves, he feels inspired to go back to his own kitchen and experiment. This Asian Coleslaw was created in this manner, with the professional critique of Chef Dave Dewhirst of Sushi Metsuyan and The Pasta Factory in Teaneck.

Black Bean and Quinoa Salad

SERVES: 4 | PREP TIME: 10 MINUTES PLUS OVERNIGHT SOAKING TIME | COOK TIME: 40 MINUTES

- **½ cup dried black beans, soaked overnight in cold water**
- **½ cup quinoa, rinsed well**
- **½ teaspoon salt, divided**
- **½ cup frozen corn kernels, thawed**
- **1 jalapeño pepper, seeded and minced**
- **1 red bell pepper, ¼-inch dice**
- **½ cup loosely packed cilantro, chopped**
- **2 tablespoons extra virgin olive oil**
- **1 lime, juiced**
- **2 tablespoons balsamic vinegar**
- **freshly ground black pepper**
- **2 cherry tomatoes, quartered for garnish**

Place beans in a pot and cover with cold water. Bring to a boil and cook over medium heat for 30 minutes. Drain. Place in a bowl. Cook quinoa in ½ cup boiling water with ¼ teaspoon salt until water is absorbed, approximately 10 minutes. Cool. Add to beans along with corn, jalapeño, red bell pepper and cilantro. Stir in oil, lime juice, balsamic vinegar, remaining ¼ teaspoon salt and pepper to taste.

TO PLATE: *Spoon into a serving bowl and garnish with tomatoes. Serve at room temperature.*

NOTE: *Protein rich and lower in carbohydrates than most grains, quinoa is technically not a grain at all, but rather a seed. With its interesting taste and nice texture, it transforms any dish into something wonderful. Be sure to rinse the quinoa well before cooking it to wash away any bitter powder on the seeds.*

Beans need to be rinsed before soaking. Discard any small rocks, shriveled beans and dirt. The main reason to soak beans is to shorten the cooking time. If you are not able to soak the beans overnight, a quick soak is done by covering the beans with water to 2 inches above beans in a large pot. When water comes to a boil, reduce heat and simmer for 2 minutes. Remove from heat; cover and let stand 1 hour, then drain. Do not add salt or acidic ingredients, such as tomatoes, vinegar or citrus to beans until they are tender; cooking in salted water toughens the beans and acid prevents the beans from becoming tender. Cook beans at a simmer, not at a boil, as boiling causes the skin to split. Store uncooked beans in an airtight container, in a cool, dry place for up to 1 year. Do not store in the refrigerator where they can absorb moisture and spoil.

Helen Nash, with a deep understanding of and passion for food, continues to educate the public. Her recipes are never difficult. Flavors are combined to enhance the featured item, never to mask it. One of her many talents is the ability to show home cooks how to truly enjoy the process of cooking, emphasizing simplicity, good health and freshness. She is the author of *Kosher Cuisine, Helen Nash's Kosher Kitchen* and *Helen Nash's Lower Fat Kosher Kitchen.* She also writes a food column, *The Chef's Table,* for the Orthodox Union's publication, *Jewish Action.*

Crunchy Chicken with Mixed Salad and Date Dressing

SERVES: 6 | PREP TIME: 15 MINUTES PLUS OVERNIGHT MARINATING AND ADDITIONAL 2 HOURS REFRIGERATION | COOK TIME: 15 MINUTES

CHICKEN

- **⅓ cup extra virgin olive oil**
- **⅓ cup lemon juice**
- **1 tablespoon chopped fresh rosemary**
- **5 thyme sprigs, using leaves only**
- **1 pound chicken cutlets cut into strips, 3-inch long, ¾-inch wide, 1-inch thick**
- **3 egg whites**
- **3 tablespoons soy sauce**
- **5 tablespoons cornmeal**
- **¼ cup peanut or canola oil, plus more if needed for frying**

DRESSING

- **2 tablespoons date spread**
- **½ cup lemon juice**
- **½ cup extra virgin olive oil**
- **salt and freshly ground black pepper**

SALAD

- **1 head romaine or red leaf lettuce, torn into bite-size pieces**
- **3 cucumbers, peeled and cut into small cubes**
- **2 carrots, peeled and cut into small sticks**
- **½ pint cherry tomatoes, halved**
- **5 mushrooms, sliced**
- **1 medium-size red onion, thinly sliced**
- **4 small radishes, thinly sliced**
- **1 avocado, peeled, pitted and cubed**
- **2 oranges, peeled and segmented**
- **4 dried dates, thickly sliced**
- **2 ounces soy nuts**

In a medium bowl, combine oil, lemon juice, rosemary and thyme. Add chicken and marinate overnight in refrigerator. The following day, in a clean bowl, beat egg whites until just beginning to stiffen. Fold in soy sauce and cornmeal. Add chicken; refrigerate 2 hours.

In a small bowl, prepare dressing by whisking date spread, lemon juice, oil, salt and pepper to taste.

Heat oil in a frying pan. Carefully add chicken pieces in a single layer, cooking for 2-3 minutes on each side. Drain.

Place lettuce, cucumbers, carrots, tomatoes, mushrooms, onion, radishes, avocado, oranges and dates in a large bowl; add enough dressing to coat and toss well.

TO PLATE: *Place salad on a plate; top with chicken pieces, drizzle with dressing and sprinkle with soy nuts.*

Twenty years ago Naomi and Eric Goldberg, originally from Manchester, England, chose to make Israel their home. Who would have believed that the aromas emanating from their first kitchenette in the Absorption Center, would lead to Naomi Catering, which now resides in a two-story commissary, and whose reputation spreads across five continents! The Goldbergs' customers appreciate quality, punctuality, attention to detail and overall service.

Roasted Portobello Mushrooms and Baby Arugula Salad

SERVES: 6-8 | PREP TIME: 15 MINUTES | COOK TIME: 30 MINUTES

SALAD

- 3 large portobello mushroom caps
- olive oil for drizzling
- salt and freshly ground black pepper
- 3 sprigs fresh thyme
- 1 (6-ounce) bunch baby arugula, thick stems discarded
- ¼ cup thinly sliced red onion

CROUTONS

- 1 (12-ounce) challah bread, crust removed
- ¼ cup olive oil
- 1 teaspoon minced garlic
- ½ teaspoon salt

DRESSING

- ½ teaspoon mayonnaise
- ¼ cup red wine vinegar
- ½ cup canola oil
- ⅛ teaspoon extra virgin olive oil
- ¼ teaspoon minced fresh garlic
- salt and freshly ground black pepper

GARNISH

- 1-2 ounces enoki mushrooms
- ¼ cup chopped chives

Chef Michael Gershkovich of Mike's Bistro, trained at the Culinary Institute of America in Hyde Park, New York. He honed his skills at Greystone Wine Spectator Restaurant in Napa, California, the Park Avenue Café in New York and as the Executive Chef at The Prime Grill. This is an adaptation of a recipe that was demonstrated by the chef.

Preheat oven to 450 degrees. Sprinkle portobello mushrooms on both sides with oil, salt and pepper. Place thyme sprigs on a jelly roll pan topped by mushrooms, gill side down. Roast until mushrooms release their juices, about 12 minutes; turn over and continue to cook an additional 2 minutes. Reserve liquid that has been created by the mushrooms for the dressing. After cooling, thinly slice mushrooms.

To make croutons, reduce oven temperature to 350 degrees. Slice challah into ½-inch thick slices, then into ½-inch cubes. Place cubes on a jelly roll pan and toss with oil, garlic and salt. Bake 10-15 minutes, tossing periodically until croutons are golden brown.

To prepare dressing, dice some portobello mushroom slices measuring ¾ cup. Put mayonnaise, vinegar, reserved mushroom cooking liquid and diced mushrooms into a blender. Add canola oil, olive oil and garlic. Season with salt and pepper to taste. Add enough water to dressing to achieve desired consistency. Place arugula, red onion and remaining sliced mushrooms into a bowl. Add enough dressing to coat.

TO PLATE: *Place salad on individual serving dish. Garnish with enoki mushrooms, chopped chives and croutons. Serve extra dressing on the side.*

NOTE: *The crouton recipe will yield about 6 cups. For the salad, you will need 1-1½ cups. Store remaining croutons in an air-tight container and use with your favorite salad.*

Portobello mushrooms are actually mature cremini mushrooms and have a dense meaty texture when cooked. The portobello mushroom's tough woody stem is usually covered with dirt and needs to be trimmed or removed. Some chefs will also remove the gills from the underside of the cap. This is best done by using a spoon, working from the center downward, giving the cap a quarter turn and repeating the process all the way around.

Enoki mushrooms, because of the manner in which they are cultivated, are long, thin-stemmed, small, white mushrooms. With their fruity flavor and crisp texture, they are usually served raw or barely cooked and make an attractive garnish.

salad dressings

Vinaigrette Dressing

Carmel Spa's Lemon Dressing

Italian Dressing

Roasted Garlic Dressing

Horseradish Dressing

French Dressing

Blue Cheese Dressing

Creamy Dressing

Dairy Caesar Salad Dressing

Non-Dairy Caesar Salad Dressing

Salad Dressings

Manufacturers of bottled dressings are forced to add emulsifiers, stabilizers and preservatives to keep their product stable for long periods of time. A chef prefers to make fresh dressing, using only the best ingredients. These dressings are from our own collection of favorites.

Vinaigrette Dressing

YIELD: 1¾ CUPS

¼ cup Dijon mustard
½ cup red wine vinegar
1 teaspoon minced shallots
1 teaspoon minced garlic
1¼ cups extra virgin olive oil

Put mustard, vinegar, shallots and garlic in a blender; blend 15 seconds. With motor running, drizzle in oil and continue to blend until dressing is creamy.

Carmel Spa's Lemon Dressing

YIELD: 1 CUP

⅓ cup lemon juice
⅓ cup water
⅓ cup extra virgin olive oil
2 teaspoons honey
1 teaspoon mustard
1 garlic clove, chopped
½ teaspoon dried tarragon
salt and freshly ground black pepper

In a bowl, whisk lemon juice, water, oil, honey, mustard, garlic, tarragon, salt and pepper to taste.

Italian Dressing

YIELD: 1¼ CUPS

¼ cup red wine vinegar
1 tablespoon lemon juice
1 teaspoon minced garlic
¼ cup water
1¼ teaspoons salt
¼ teaspoon ground black pepper
¼ teaspoon chopped oregano
¼ teaspoon chopped thyme
¼ teaspoon sugar
¾ cup extra virgin olive oil

In a small bowl, whisk vinegar, lemon juice, garlic, water, salt, pepper, oregano, thyme, sugar and oil.

Roasted Garlic Dressing

YIELD: 1 CUP

1 head garlic
2 tablespoons extra virgin olive oil
salt
¼ cup balsamic vinegar
2 teaspoons water
½ teaspoon Dijon mustard
¼ teaspoon salt
⅛ teaspoon ground black pepper
1 teaspoon sugar
½ cup extra virgin olive oil
salt and freshly ground black pepper

To roast garlic, preheat oven to 400 degrees. Cut head of garlic in half cross-wise. Drizzle with 2 tablespoons oil and sprinkle with salt. Wrap each half in its own foil. Roast in oven 1 hour; cool slightly in foil. Squeeze garlic out of skins into blender or food processor. Add vinegar, water, mustard, salt, pepper and sugar. Turn blender on; gradually add oil until emulsified. Season to taste with salt and pepper.

Horseradish Dressing

YIELD: ¾ CUP

- **½ cup mayonnaise**
- **2 tablespoons prepared red horseradish**
- **3 tablespoons sour pickle juice**
- **2 teaspoons minced garlic**
- **1 tablespoon chopped dill**
- **½ teaspoon sugar**
- **¼ teaspoon salt**

In a small bowl, whisk mayonnaise, horseradish, pickle juice, garlic, dill, sugar and salt.

French Dressing

YIELD: 1¼ CUPS

- **1 clove garlic, minced**
- **¼ cup chili sauce**
- **¼ teaspoon salt**
- **¼ teaspoon mustard**
- **¼ cup white vinegar**
- **¼ cup sugar**
- **¼ teaspoon paprika**
- **¼ teaspoon Worcestershire sauce**
- **¾ cup extra virgin olive oil**

In a blender or food processor, blend garlic, chili sauce, salt, mustard, vinegar, sugar, paprika, Worcestershire sauce and oil until combined, about 30 seconds.

salad dressings

Blue Cheese Dressing

YIELD: ¾ CUP

- **½ cup light mayonnaise**
- **½ cup fat free sour cream**
- **1 tablespoon red wine vinegar**
- **¼ teaspoon Dijon mustard**
- **1 teaspoon minced garlic**
- **4 ounces blue cheese, crumbled**

In a small bowl, whisk mayonnaise, sour cream, vinegar and mustard. Stir in garlic and blue cheese.

Creamy Dressing

YIELD: ¼ CUP

- **¼ cup mayonnaise**
- **4 teaspoons red wine vinegar**
- **1 clove garlic, minced**
- **½ teaspoon salt**
- **½ teaspoon sugar**

In a small bowl, whisk mayonnaise, vinegar, garlic, salt and sugar until creamy.

Dairy Caesar Salad Dressing

YIELD: 1¼ CUPS

- **1 clove garlic**
- **¼ cup grated Swiss or Parmesan cheese**
- **⅔ cup extra virgin olive oil**
- **3 tablespoons cottage cheese**
- **1 teaspoon salt**
- **2 teaspoons sugar**
- **¼ cup apple cider vinegar**

Put garlic, Swiss or Parmesan cheese, oil, cottage cheese, salt, sugar and vinegar into a food processor or blender. Process until smooth.

Non-Dairy Caesar Salad Dressing

YIELD: ¾ CUP

- ½ **lemon, juiced**
- ¼ **cup extra virgin olive oil**
- 1 **tablespoon chopped garlic**
- 3 **drops Worcestershire sauce**
- 3 **tablespoons mayonnaise**
- ½ **teaspoon Dijon mustard**
- 1 **tablespoon sugar**
- 1 **tablespoon chopped parsley**
- ⅛ **teaspoon salt**
- ⅛ **teaspoon ground black pepper**

In a bowl, whisk lemon juice, oil, garlic, Worcestershire sauce, mayonnaise, mustard, sugar, parsley, salt and pepper.

NOTE: *A dressing should not overpower a salad, but rather enhance it. The flavor intensity of the greens and any accompaniments, as well as the flavor of the dressing itself, will dictate the amount of dressing that is used. As a general rule of thumb, a salad composed of greens should be served with crisp ingredients. To maintain this texture, the greens are placed in a mixing bowl immediately before serving and the dressing is added just to the point of lightly coating. Avoid a salad that is swimming in dressing. Salads comprised of non-leafy ingredients, such as mushrooms, can be dressed in advance so that the flavors can meld. These dressings can be used with a variety of ingredients. They should be stored covered and refrigerated. Refrigeration will cause the oil to solidify. Therefore, allow the dressing to liquefy by sitting at room temperature prior to using.*

meat

Steak with Sweet Heat

Grilled Veal Chop with Quince Compote

Standing Rib Roast and
Elegant Tomato with Basil

Herbed Baby Lamb Chops
with Moroccan Stuffed Figs

Cumin Cilantro Skirt Steak
with Chimichurri Sauce

Lamb or Veal Osso Buco with
Gremolata, Potato and Root Vegetables

Grilled Boneless Rib Eye Steak with
Homemade Red and Yellow Ketchups

Perfect Char-Grilled Burgers
with Freshly Baked Buns

Steak au Poivre with Pommes Frites

Grilled Marinated London Broil

Steak with Sweet Heat

SERVES: 4 | PREP TIME: 15 MINUTES | COOK TIME: 45 MINUTES

STEAKS

4 (8-ounce) rib steaks

SPICE RUB

2 teaspoons chili powder

2 teaspoons Spanish paprika

2 teaspoons ground cumin

2 teaspoons ground coriander

2 teaspoons dry mustard

2 teaspoons dried oregano

1 teaspoon kosher salt

1 teaspoon ground black pepper

CARAMELIZED ONIONS

2 tablespoons margarine

1 tablespoon canola oil

3 large Spanish onions, halved and thinly sliced into half moons

1 teaspoon kosher salt

¼ teaspoon ground black pepper

FIERY DRESSING

¼ cup red wine vinegar

2 cloves garlic, chopped

1 jalapeño pepper

2 teaspoons honey

¼ teaspoon kosher salt

¼ teaspoon ground black pepper

½ cup canola oil

¼ cup finely chopped fresh cilantro leaves

Remove steaks from refrigerator. In a small bowl, combine chili powder, paprika, cumin, coriander, mustard, oregano, salt and pepper. Set aside.

For caramelized onions, heat margarine and oil in a large sauté pan over medium heat. Add onion and season with salt and pepper. Cook slowly until golden brown, stirring occasionally, approximately 35 minutes.

For dressing, combine vinegar, garlic, jalapeño, honey, salt and pepper in a blender until smooth. Slowly drizzle in oil and blend until emulsified. Add cilantro and pulse 2 times just to incorporate.

In a small bowl, combine avocado, red onion, lime juice, oil, oregano, salt and pepper. Preheat broiler. Rub one side of each steak with spice rub and drizzle tops with oil. Place steaks in broiler pan, rub-side up and place under broiler. Broil until top of steak is golden brown and slightly charred, about 6 minutes. Turn steak over and continue broiling to medium-rare doneness, approximately 6 additional minutes. Remove and let rest 5 minutes before serving.

TO PLATE: *Ladle dressing onto a large dinner plate. Place steak on top of dressing with some of the caramelized onions. Garnish with avocado-oregano relish.*

NOTE: *Spicy, sweet, tangy — all on one plate! Although the original recipe calls for a cheese sauce and is billed as Philadelphia Style Steak at Bobby Flay Steak in Atlantic City, a different relish has been substituted. The relish remains true to Bobby's credo of influencing what we eat with bold flavors and big ideas.*

Rib steaks are always a favorite cut of meat. Greater marbling gives the steak flavor and rich texture. To determine when a steak is done, press it with your index finger. A rare steak will be soft; medium will be firm but yielding, well-done will be firm. Always allow meat to rest for 5 minutes before serving, as this will allow

AVOCADO-OREGANO RELISH

- 2 ripe Haas avocados, pitted, peeled and coarsely chopped
- ½ medium-size red onion, finely chopped
- 2 limes, juiced
- 2 tablespoons canola oil
- 1 tablespoon finely chopped fresh oregano leaves
- ¼ teaspoon kosher salt
- ¼ teaspoon ground black pepper
- 2 tablespoons canola oil

the juices to evenly distribute. For medium-rare, 1-inch thick steak will need to cook for approximately 12 minutes, 1½-inch thick for 16 minutes, and 2-inch for 18 minutes total cooking time.

Haas avocados are the small brown ones from California. The green ones are not as flavorful.

Bobby Flay's culinary versatility is evident in the multiple talents he brings to the field: critically-acclaimed chef/restaurateur, award-winning cookbook author and television personality. Flay began working in a kitchen at age 17 and afterwards received a formal education at The French Culinary Institute. Flay credits Wolfgang Puck and Jonathan Waxman for proving that food does not "have to be fussy; it can be delicious and creative while embracing great colors and textures." Flay defines this theme by drawing exclusively from regional ingredients, then rejuvenating old classics and celebrating diversity.

Grilled Veal Chop with Quince Compote

SERVES: 4 | PREP TIME: 20 MINUTES, PLUS 2 HOURS FOR BRINING | COOK TIME: 45 MINUTES

VEAL CHOPS AND BRINE

- 1 gallon water
- ½ cup sugar
- ¼ cup kosher salt
- 2 carrots, sliced ⅛-inch thick
- 1 medium onion, sliced
- 10 juniper berries
- 3 fresh bay leaves
- 4 (12-ounce, 1¼-inch thick) veal rib chops
- 2 teaspoons olive oil
- ⅛ teaspoon ground black pepper

To make brine, bring water to a boil with sugar, salt, carrots, onion, juniper berries and bay leaves. Cook until salt and sugar dissolve. Cool to room temperature and add chops to brine; soak in refrigerator for 2 hours. Remove from brine and pat dry. To grill, brush chops with oil, sprinkle with a little pepper and place on a hot, oiled grill. Grill 5-7 minutes per side for medium-rare.

COMPOTE

- 4 cups red wine
- 4 quinces, peeled, cored, cut into ¼-inch thick pieces
- 1 tablespoon olive oil
- 2 cups peeled and sliced shallots
- ¼ cup red wine vinegar
- 3 tablespoons honey
- salt and freshly ground black pepper

For compote, add wine and quince to a pot. Add enough water so fruit is completely covered with liquid. Simmer until fruit is tender, approximately 15 minutes. Separate fruit from liquid; reduce liquid over medium heat to a syrup consistency, which should coat the back of a spoon. In a sauté pan, heat oil. Add shallots, cooking and constantly mixing until caramelized. Add vinegar and honey. Cook until shallots are glazed with honey vinegar over medium heat, about 8 minutes. Combine glazed shallots, reduced wine syrup and quince. Adjust seasoning with salt and pepper to taste.

GARNISH

- canola oil for frying
- 1 large shallot, thinly sliced
- ¼ cup all purpose flour
- salt and freshly ground black pepper
- 1 teaspoon margarine
- 12 baby assorted color carrots with tops, peeled and tops trimmed to ¼-inch

Heat a frying pan with oil over medium heat. Toss shallot with flour in a bowl, to coat. Shake to remove excess flour. Add shallot to hot oil and cook until golden brown, about 2 minutes. Remove shallot with a slotted spoon, drain on paper towel and sprinkle with salt and pepper. Set aside. For carrots, prepare a bowl of ice cold water. In a saucepan with salted boiling water, cook carrots 4 minutes or until barely tender. Transfer carrots to ice water and drain in a colander. When ready to serve, in a non-stick skillet, heat margarine over medium heat. Add carrots to skillet to warm. Season to taste with salt and pepper.

TO PLATE: *Spoon the savory compote on a plate and prop the chop against the compote. The bone should be pointing upwards for vertical height. Drape chop with a few fried shallots. Serve with carrots.*

NOTE: *The ancient fruit quince, with its astringent tart flavor is inedible in its raw state. It is a fall favorite, reminiscent of the eastern Mediterranean region and North Africa, where sour fruit is paired with grilled meats.*

Before the chef grills the veal chops, he brines them for succulence and flavor. Juniper berries are one component of the brine. Unlike herbs, which come mostly from leaves and stems, spices may come from roots, bark, flower buds, fruits or seeds of aromatic plants. Spices are used in small quantities to enhance the subtlety of the dish, not drown the inherent flavors of the foods being prepared. Juniper berries, about the size of peppercorns, come from a small evergreen tree. They are available dried in the spice section of your market.

The chef plates the veal with baby, mixed-colored carrots which, although not as common, can be purchased at specialty produce markets in orange, purple, maroon, yellow and white, adding color, taste and interest to the dish.

Todd Aarons, Executive Chef of Tierra Sur, is a graduate of the California Culinary Academy. He further developed his culinary craft under Judy Rogers at Zuni Café; at Savoy in New York City; in Tuscany; and at Beringer Vineyard's School for American Chefs. Then, while consulting for cafes in Israel, he became interested in the dietary laws of kashrut. Following this miraculous trip, he devoted himself to creating the highest levels of kosher cuisine available. Prior to joining Tierra Sur, which received acclaims for being "one of the best restaurants" by the *Los Angeles Times,* Chef Aarons opened his own upscale glatt kosher French Mediterranean restaurant, Mosaica, in New Jersey.

Standing Rib Roast and Elegant Tomato with Basil

SERVES: 6 | PREP TIME: 25 MINUTES, PLUS 2 HOURS REFRIGERATION | COOK TIME: 2 HOURS PLUS 25 MINUTES FOR RESTING

RIB ROAST

- 5 cloves garlic, peeled
- 1 shallot, peeled and quartered
- 2 tablespoons olive oil
- 2 teaspoons dried basil
- 2 teaspoons dried rosemary
- 2 teaspoons dried thyme
- 1½ teaspoons kosher salt
- 2 teaspoons ground black pepper
- 1 (4 to 5-pound) standing rib roast

ELEGANT TOMATO WITH BASIL

- 6 large beefsteak or vine-ripened tomatoes
- salt and freshly ground black pepper
- rice vinegar
- 2 cups basil leaves, divided
- ½ cup extra virgin olive oil
- fleur de sel
- 6 basil sprigs for garnish

In a food processor, chop garlic and shallot; add oil, basil, rosemary, thyme, salt and pepper. Pulse once. Pat meat dry and place in a roasting pan at least 3 inches deep, bone-side down. Using your hands, spread rub all over outside of meat. Cover and refrigerate 2 hours. To cook meat, remove from refrigerator; allow roast to come to room temperature, covered. If you skip this step the roast will not cook evenly. Preheat oven to 400 degrees. Roast 30 minutes. Decrease heat to 350 degrees and roast an additional 1½ hours. Internal temperature, measured by a meat thermometer should be 120 degrees for rare, 125 degrees for medium-rare. Remove and allow to rest, tented with foil, for 25 minutes.

To peel tomatoes, drop tomatoes into a pot of boiling water, removing them when skins loosen, after about 30 seconds, using a slotted spoon. Place tomatoes immediately into ice cold water. When cool, peel. Cut a thin slice off top and bottom of tomato. Cut remainder of tomato into 4 horizontal slices, keeping slices in order. Between each slice, sprinkle salt, pepper and a few drops of vinegar. To prepare basil oil, place 1 cup basil leaves into boiling water for 10 seconds, remove and rinse immediately in ice cold water. Place them, still wet, in a food processor. With motor running, drizzle in oil. Do not blend too much or oil will turn olive color, rather than being a bright green. Season with salt. Re-assemble tomatoes inserting a basil leaf between each slice. Set aside. Remove bones from meat and slice.

TO PLATE: *Serve 1 slice of meat accompanied by tomato. Drizzle basil oil onto tomato. Sprinkle tomato and meat with fleur de sel. Put basil sprig on top of tomato to resemble stem.*

NOTE: *"Standing" rib roast indicates that the rib bones are left intact and the roast is cooked standing on its rack of ribs. The attached rib bones provide greater moisture retention, more flavor and act as a natural roasting rack. This is considered to be one of the most elegant cuts of beef. It is tender, flavorful and expensive. For a perfectly cooked rib roast, invest in a meat thermometer. Internal temperature, not time, is the best test for doneness.*

Fleur de sel is one of four common varieties of salt. It is obtained by hand-harvesting crystals that form on the surface of a salt marsh and then is left to dry in the sun. As a result of its higher mineral content, fleur de sel has a delicious ocean aroma. It is used as a condiment, adding both texture and flavor to the food it enhances.

Jean-Georges Vongerichten was born and raised in France. As a young boy, he quickly became known as "the palate," tasting and making recommendations to his mother and grandmother who would prepare lunch for 50 employees. After a formal culinary training, he opened ten restaurants around the world, gaining exposure to all types of cuisine, including Asian, whereby he developed his fusion style. At the age of 29, he received four stars from the *New York Times,* crediting him for his "vibrant, explosive, flavorful take-your-breath-away food." Aside from authoring two cookbooks, he takes pride in his restaurant accomplishments: Vong, JoJo, Jean-Georges Restaurant, The Mercer Kitchen, 66, Nougatine and Spice Market, located in New York. Chef Jean-Georges has given us the accompanying tomato basil recipe from his book, *Jean-Georges Cooking at Home with a Four-Star Chef* (Broadway Books).

Herbed Baby Lamb Chops with Moroccan Stuffed Figs

SERVES: 6 | PREP TIME: 10 MINUTES PLUS OVERNIGHT MARINATING | COOK TIME: 15 MINUTES

LAMB

12 baby lamb chops

1 tablespoon rosemary leaves

2 tablespoons thyme leaves

6 garlic cloves, smashed

2 teaspoons salt

¾ cup olive oil

FIGS STUFFED WITH COUSCOUS AND CRANBERRY

⅓ cup couscous

½ cup boiling salted water

1¼ teaspoons extra virgin olive oil, divided

¼ cup dried cranberries

½ cup grated carrots

1 tablespoon diced red onion

1 tablespoon chopped cilantro

2 tablespoons chopped pecans

6 fresh ripe figs

Season lamb with rosemary, thyme, garlic, salt and oil. Cover and refrigerate overnight. Prior to cooking the lamb, remove it from refrigerator, allowing it to come to room temperature.

Meanwhile, to prepare figs, add couscous to boiling salted water; add 1 teaspoon oil. Cover; remove from heat. Let stand 5 minutes. Add cranberries, carrots, onion, cilantro, pecans and remaining ¼ teaspoon oil. Halve figs; scoop out some of the fruit, leaving outside shell intact. Chop fig fruit that has been removed and add to couscous. Heap couscous mixture into fig shells; set aside.

Cook lamb by broiling 4 minutes per side for medium-rare or adjust time for desired degree of doneness. The inside should remain pink.

TO PLATE: *Serve 2 lamb chops criss-crossed accompanied by two fig halves. Spoon pan juices over lamb chops.*

NOTE: *Incorporating fresh figs as an accompaniment to this savory dish adds the perfect sweet compliment. When purchasing, select ripe figs that are heavy, soft, plump and rich in color. Figs are highly perishable; avoid washing until just before serving.*

Ask your butcher to French trim the baby lamb chops, scraping the lamb bones clean.

Marty Levin, a graduate of the Culinary Institute of America, now the Executive Chef for Celebration Caterers in New York, never ceases to impress his guests, tantalizing their taste buds with new sensations. He accomplishes this goal with his award-winning culinary team.

Cumin Cilantro Skirt Steak with Chimichurri Sauce

SERVES: 4 | PREP TIME: 10 MINUTES PLUS 2 HOURS SOAKING AND OVERNIGHT MARINATING | COOK TIME: 10 MINUTES

STEAK

1½ pounds skirt steak

1 tablespoon ground cumin

3 garlic cloves, chopped

1½ teaspoons red pepper flakes

½ cup chopped cilantro

¼ cup fresh lime juice

½ cup olive oil

CHIMICHURRI SAUCE

6 cloves garlic, minced

2 jalapeño peppers, seeded and minced

¼ cup red wine vinegar

½ cup finely chopped fresh flat-leaf parsley

½ cup finely chopped fresh oregano leaves

4 limes, juiced

1 cup extra virgin olive oil

1 teaspoon salt

1 teaspoon ground black pepper

Soak meat in cold water for 2 hours to decrease saltiness. Drain and pat dry. In a small bowl, combine cumin, garlic, red pepper flakes, cilantro, lime juice and oil. Place meat in large sealable plastic bag. Pour marinade into bag, seal and refrigerate overnight.

To make chimichurri, in a bowl, combine garlic, jalapeño, vinegar, parsley, oregano and lime juice. Whisk in oil and season with salt and pepper. Set aside at room temperature to allow flavors to meld.

Remove meat from refrigerator. Heat grill. When very hot, remove meat from marinade and place on grill; discard marinade. Grill meat 5 minutes on each side. Remove to a cutting board and allow to rest for 5 minutes. Slice.

TO PLATE: *Fan sliced steak on a plate. Spoon some chimichurri sauce over meat. Serve with remaining sauce on the side.*

NOTE: *Because skirt steak is thin, it absorbs more salt than other cuts of meat during the koshering process. To remove some of the saltiness it requires soaking, which is not necessary for other meat.*

Chimichurri is a thick herb sauce and marinade, served at room temperature on grilled meat. It is as common in Latin America as ketchup is in America. It is said that Jimmy McCurry, an Irishman who was sympathetic to the cause of Argentina's Independence in the 19th century, is credited for being the sauce's creator. His name was difficult for the natives to pronounce and evolved into chimichurri.

There is no better way to ignite a charcoal grill than with a metal chimney starter, which can be inexpensively purchased in a hardware store. Roll up 3 or 4 pages of newspaper, put them in the bottom of the chimney starter, add charcoal and light the newspaper. In 15 minutes, you have a hot grill without any taste of lighter fluid. Remove meat from refrigerator 20 minutes before grilling. When you put the steaks on the grill, the grill should be very hot. Allow the steaks to cook undisturbed! Do not push them down or move them around. By leaving them alone, the meat will not stick or lose valuable juices. Additionally, the goal is to develop grill marks and a strong caramelized flavor. Skirt steak is not a melt-in-your-mouth type of steak. It is a perfect cut of meat to marinade. It should be chewy, not tough, with a lot of character.

Almost a decade ago, Tobi and Lauren Cleaver, defense attorneys in Colorado, longed for a different life somewhere in the tropics where life was simple. Their dream came to fruition when they became the owners of the Iguana Lodge, deep in the Costa Rican Rainforest on the Osa Peninsula. Living there, they learned a phrase that is used in everyday speech — "pura vida" — roughly translated to mean "pure life." The people of Costa Rica incorporate these words into a life philosophy of valuing the simple things. In the evenings at the Iguana Lodge, under a thatched roof, illuminated by dozens of candles, guests savor a dining experience in one of the most spectacular settings. Pura Vida!

Lamb or Veal Osso Buco with Gremolata, Potato and Root Vegetables

SERVES: 6 | PREP TIME: 25 MINUTES PLUS OVERNIGHT REFRIGERATION | COOK TIME: 3 HOURS

LAMB OR VEAL SHANKS

- **¼ cup olive oil, divided**
- **2 Vidalia onions, chopped**
- **1 carrot, chopped**
- **2 celery stalks, chopped**
- **2 tablespoons chopped fresh rosemary or 2 teaspoons dried**
- **6 cloves garlic, chopped**
- **6 (10-ounce) lamb or veal shanks**
- **salt and freshly ground black pepper**
- **3 cups dry red wine, divided**
- **3 cups beef broth**
- **½ cup canned diced tomatoes**
- **2 bay leaves**

Heat 2 tablespoons oil in a large, heavy-duty braising pot or Dutch oven over medium-high heat. Add onions, carrot and celery. Stir often, sautéing 10 minutes. Add rosemary and garlic; sauté 1 minute. Transfer to a bowl. Using same pot, heat remaining 2 tablespoons oil over high heat. Lightly season meat with salt and pepper. Add shanks to oil in batches. Turn over with tongs, cooking until brown on all sides, about 10 minutes per batch. Do not crowd meat or rush this searing step. Remove shanks. Add 1 cup wine to pot, scraping up any browned bits as this is where much of the flavor lies. Add sautéed vegetables to pot along with remaining 2 cups wine, broth, tomatoes and bay leaves; bring to a boil. Add lamb shanks. Reduce heat, cover and simmer 1½ hours. Uncover and cook an additional 1 hour. Allow to cool, then refrigerate overnight. Skim off hardened fat. Heat just until sauce is warm. Discard bay leaves. Remove shanks. Purée sauce in a blender or food processor; return back to pot with shanks. Heat. Adjust seasoning with salt and pepper to taste.

POTATO AND ROOT VEGETABLES

- **2 Yukon potatoes (1¼ pounds), peeled and cut into 2-inch pieces**
- **1 rutabaga (about 1 pound), peeled, halved and cut into 2-inch pieces**
- **3 small parsnips (about ½ pound), peeled and cut into 2-inch pieces**
- **1½ tablespoons extra virgin olive oil**
- **salt and freshly ground black pepper**

To prepare potato and root vegetables, bring large pot of salted water to a boil. Add potatoes, rutabaga and parsnips. Boil until vegetables are tender, about 30 minutes. Drain. Return vegetables to same pot. With a potato masher, mash, leaving some texture. Mix in oil. Season with salt and pepper to taste.

GREMOLATA

3 **tablespoons chopped fresh flat-leaf parsley**

1 **large garlic clove, minced**

3 **tablespoons grated lemon zest**

For gremolata, in a small bowl, combine parsley, garlic and lemon zest.

TO PLATE: *For each serving, arrange a cushion of mashed root vegetables on a warm plate. Top with lamb or veal shank. Sprinkle with gremolata and ladle sauce along edge of plate.*

NOTE: *The term braising refers to a dish that is cooked, covered in liquid, just below the boiling point. Osso Buco is a classic braised dish from Northern Italy. It tastes even better the day after it is cooked because flavors have time to develop and it is less fatty (because hardened fat, which is created when the dish is refrigerated overnight, is easier to remove). As is the tradition, it is garnished with gremolata, a condiment composed of lemon zest, parsley and garlic. This is a memorable meal for any lamb or veal lover.*

A fabulous home cook shared this recipe with us. Although the recipe is lengthy, she asserted that, without a doubt, it is the best meal she makes.

Grilled Boneless Rib Eye Steak with Homemade Red and Yellow Ketchups

SERVES: 6 | PREP TIME: 10 MINUTES, PLUS 1 HOUR MARINATING | COOK TIME: 1¼ HOURS

STEAK

- **6 (6-ounce, 2-inch) boneless rib eye steaks**
- **1 cup balsamic vinegar**
- **¼ cup olive oil**
- **2 teaspoons minced fresh garlic**
- **1 teaspoon salt**

RED TOMATO KETCHUP

- **¼ cup brown sugar**
- **3 tablespoons chopped shallots**
- **¾ teaspoon minced fresh garlic**
- **¼ red bell pepper, halved and chopped**
- **1½ cups canned diced tomatoes in heavy purée**
- **3 tablespoons red wine vinegar**
- **1 tablespoon balsamic vinegar**
- **⅛ teaspoon cayenne pepper sauce**

YELLOW PEPPER KETCHUP

- **2 large yellow bell peppers, halved**
- **1½ teaspoons minced fresh garlic**
- **3 tablespoons red wine vinegar**
- **3 tablespoons sugar**
- **¼ cup coarsely chopped shallots**

GARNISH

- **6 small lettuce leaves**

Owners/chefs, Johanne Killeen and George Germon of Al Forno in Providence, Rhode Island, have won many awards for their superb cooking and down-to-earth style. This recipe has been adapted from their book *Cucina Simpatica* (Harper Collins Publishers).

With kitchen twine, tie 2 strings, parallel to each other, around outer edge of each steak to form a round shape. Place steaks in a baking dish. Combine vinegar, oil, garlic and salt and pour over steaks; cover and marinate in refrigerator 1 hour.

Meanwhile, prepare ketchups. For red ketchup, melt sugar in a saucepan over medium heat, stirring constantly for about 3 minutes. Add shallots, garlic and red bell pepper. Cook 3 minutes. Add tomatoes, red wine and balsamic vinegars. Bring to a boil. Reduce heat and simmer 25 minutes. Purée in a food processor until smooth; add pepper sauce. For yellow ketchup, purée yellow bell peppers, garlic, vinegar, sugar and shallots in food processor until smooth. Pour into a sauce pan and bring to a boil. Reduce heat and simmer 30 minutes. Allow to reach room temperature and refrigerate. When ready to serve, remove steaks from refrigerator and allow to come to room temperature. Heat a grill until very hot. Place steaks on grate and grill 8 minutes, without disturbing. Turn and grill an additional 8 minutes for medium-rare. Transfer to a warm platter and allow to rest 8 minutes before serving. Remove strings.

TO PLATE: *Serve steak on a plate garnished with lettuce leaf accompanied by two ketchups.*

NOTE: *Rib eye, because of its flavor and texture, is considered to be the favorite cut of meat for most butchers. This cut of meat can be purchased bone-in or boneless.*

One way to determine if a grill is hot enough is to place your hand 3 inches above the heat. If you cannot keep your hand there for more than 3 seconds, then the grill is ready.

Resting meat after steaks are cooked makes the meat more juicy and tender. Ketchups can be stored in a covered container and refrigerated; red will last up to 2 weeks, yellow up to 1 week.

Perfect Char-Grilled Burgers with Freshly Baked Buns

SERVES: 6 | PREP TIME: 10 MINUTES | COOK TIME: 8 MINUTES

BURGERS

2¼ pounds chopped ground chuck meat
1½ teaspoons onion powder
1½ teaspoons garlic powder
½ teaspoon salt
¾ teaspoon ground black pepper
¼ cup ketchup
1 teaspoon soy sauce
1 tablespoon duck sauce
1½ teaspoons Caribbean jerk marinade
½ cup seasoned breadcrumbs
2 tablespoons canola oil
salt and freshly ground pepper

Heat grill. In a large bowl, handling the meat as little as possible, combine chopped chuck meat, onion powder, garlic powder, salt, pepper, ketchup, soy sauce, duck sauce, Caribbean jerk marinade and breadcrumbs. Divide meat into 6 equal portions. Form each into a ball, then gently press down, forming a disc. Rotate disc between the palm of your hands, pressing the side with your thumb to keep the disc round and the sides straight. Refrigerate until ready to grill. Brush oil onto burgers. Season with salt and pepper. Place burger, oil side down, onto hot grill. Cook over direct heat for 4 minutes. Brush top with oil and flip to other side for additional 4 minutes for medium-rare. Remove and allow to rest 5 minutes.

BUNS

YIELD: 6 | PREP TIME: 15 MINUTES PLUS 1 HOUR FOR RISING | COOK TIME: 15 MINUTES

2⅓ cups bread flour
2 teaspoons sugar
1 teaspoon instant yeast
2 large eggs, divided
2 tablespoons canola oil
¾ teaspoon salt
¾ cup warm water
1½ teaspoons sesame seeds

In a mixer, with a dough hook, combine flour, sugar and yeast. In a small bowl, combine 1 egg, oil and salt. Add to dry ingredients. Add warm water and knead for 10 minutes. Add more flour if necessary to create a dough that is soft, but not sticky. Allow to rise in a large bowl, covered with plastic wrap, in a warm place for 30 minutes. Divide dough into 6 equal balls and with your hands, press down on the dough to shape into round burger buns. Preheat oven to 375 degrees. Place shaped dough on a jelly roll pan and allow to rise 30 minutes. Brush buns with remaining lightly beaten egg. Sprinkle with sesame seeds. Bake until golden brown, about 15 minutes. Remove to rack and allow to cool.

GARNISH

6 clusters of mesclun
6 slices red onion
6 slices beefsteak tomatoes
6 pickles
ketchup
mayonnaise

Dalia Myers is known throughout many communities as the Burger Queen. Follow the instructions and you will enjoy the juiciest burger and the most fabulous, freshly baked buns you have ever tasted.

TO PLATE: *Serve burger with toasted bun, lettuce, onion, tomato, pickles, ketchup and mayonnaise.*

NOTE: *Ground chuck, coming from the neck and shoulder, is the recommended meat for this recipe. If you substitute with a cut that is too lean, the end result will be very dry and less flavorful. In general, the redder the meat, the leaner it is. The paler it is, the higher the fat content. For grilling, a fattier cut is more desirable. For meat used in meatloaf or for sautéing, a leaner cut is a better choice.*

The best way to make a patty is with your hands, but be careful not to compact the meat when shaping; overworking results in a tough burger.

The grill should be clean and very hot. Avoid moving the meat or pressing down on it with a spatula while cooking; doing so squeezes out flavorful juices.

Burgers, like steaks, should rest after they come off the heat to allow juices to redistribute throughout the meat.

Steak au Poivre with Pommes Frites

SERVES: 4 | PREP TIME: 5 MINUTES | COOK TIME: 20 MINUTES

FILET MIGNON STEAK AND SAUCE

4 (6-ounce, 1-inch thick) boneless rib eye steaks, also called filet mignon steaks

2 teaspoons kosher salt

2 tablespoons coarsely ground black peppercorns

1 tablespoon canola oil

⅓ cup minced shallots (about 1 shallot)

2 tablespoons margarine (plus 2 tablespoons margarine if using broth)

¾ cup cognac

1 cup beef broth or non-dairy cream (or non-dairy soy milk)

1 tablespoon bottled green peppercorns, slightly crushed

POMMES FRITES

2 large Idaho potatoes, peeled

peanut oil

kosher salt

Preheat oven to 200 degrees. Pat filets dry. Sprinkle both sides with salt. Press black pepper evenly on both sides. Allow to rest at room temperature.

Meanwhile, slice potatoes with a mandoline or sharp knife into thin matchsticks, ⅛-inch thick. Put matchsticks into a bowl of cold water. Pour 1 inch peanut oil into a large skillet and set over high heat. Drain and dry potatoes thoroughly. When oil is hot, add dry potatoes in batches and cook until golden brown, about 3-5 minutes. Remove with a slotted spoon and drain on paper towels. Place on a jelly roll pan. Sprinkle with salt and keep warm in oven. To cook steaks, heat a 12-inch heavy skillet over medium-high heat until hot, about 3 minutes. Add oil and swirl in skillet. Sauté steaks for 3 minutes. Turn to other side and continue to cook for 3 more minutes for medium-rare. Transfer steaks to a heatproof platter and keep warm in oven while making sauce. Pour off and discard fat from skillet. Add shallots and margarine to skillet. Cook over medium heat, stirring and scraping up brown bits, until shallots are well-browned all over, about 4 minutes. Remove pan from heat. Add cognac, return to high heat and boil, stirring until liquid is reduced to a glaze, about 3 minutes. Add broth or non-dairy cream and green peppercorns. Boil, stirring occasionally, until reduced by half, about 4-5 minutes. If using broth, add remaining 2 tablespoons margarine and cook over low heat, swirling skillet, until margarine is incorporated.

TO PLATE: *Place steak onto a nest of Pommes Frites. Top steak with sauce and a sprinkle of additional Pommes Frites.*

NOTE: *According to most kosher butchers, the filet mignon steak, also known as the eye, is the closest thing to non-kosher filet mignon. It is tender, yet juicy. When cooking the steaks, avoid using a non-stick pan. Non-stick pans prevent the caramelized brown bits from forming. It is these bits that ultimately give a sauce its fullest flavors. Anytime liquor is added, the pan is removed from the flame to prevent flare ups.*

To coarsely crack the peppercorns, place them in a small resealable plastic bag on a flat work surface. Gently tap them with the bottom of a heavy skillet, until they break into pieces.

Why does a sauce in a restaurant taste different than one made at home? In a professional kitchen, many sauces are finished with "monter au buerre," translated to mean mounting a sauce with butter. In French cooking, adding butter (in our case margarine) to a sauce finishes the sauce, allowing a creamier and mellower end result.

Raphael Bitton, originally from France, attended Yeshiva University in New York City. While there, he would frequent restaurants with his friends and was convinced that he could do better. And better he did, by opening up one of the most celebrated kosher dining houses in New York City, The Box Tree. His repertoire also includes the Bistro Grill in both Great Neck and Woodmere and a new venue in Manhattan. This adapted classic French bistro dish is, without a doubt, one of the most popular items on his restaurants' menus.

Grilled Marinated London Broil

SERVES: 6 | PREP TIME: 10 MINUTES PLUS MARINATING OVERNIGHT | COOK TIME: 20 MINUTES

- **1 small yellow onion, chopped**
- **2 cloves garlic, minced**
- **2 tablespoons fresh minced ginger**
- **1 tablespoon chopped fresh parsley**
- **1 tablespoon cumin**
- **1 tablespoon chili powder**
- **1 teaspoon dried oregano**
- **1 teaspoon turmeric**
- **1 teaspoon ground black pepper**
- **2 tablespoons soy sauce**
- **2 teaspoons sherry**
- **½ cup lemon juice**
- **½ cup olive oil**
- **1 (2½-pound, 1½-inches thick) London broil**
- **7 ounces mixed greens dressed with your favorite dressing**

In a large bowl, combine onion, garlic, ginger, parsley, cumin, chili powder, oregano, turmeric, pepper, soy sauce, sherry, lemon juice and oil. Add meat. Cover and refrigerate overnight.

Remove meat from marinade, allowing it to reach room temperature. Preheat grill until very hot. Place meat on oiled rack set about 4 inches above heat source. Grill 9-10 minutes on each side, or until meat thermometer registers 125-130 degrees for medium-rare. Alternatively, meat may be broiled. Remove from grill; let stand 10 minutes. Cut London broil diagonally across grain into thin slices.

TO PLATE: *Overlap slices of meat on a plate. Serve accompanied by dressed greens.*

NOTE: *It seems almost miraculous when a home cook uses a sharp knife for the first time. The truth is, even the best knives lose their sharpness when used regularly. Chefs hone their knives constantly, giving the knife a few strokes before each use, with the help of a sharpening steel — the metal rod that comes with most knife sets. If you examined a knife under a magnifying glass, you would see that it is comprised of hundreds of tiny teeth, like a saw. These teeth, through repeated use, get twisted and bent out of alignment. Running a knife blade over the steel, therefore, realigns the edge and makes it straight. Eventually, repeated use wears away the teeth. An abrasive stone is then necessary to create a new cutting edge. To maintain the blade's edge and for safety, knives should be stored in a wooden block instead of in a kitchen drawer.*

Cooking for Hollywood's stars, under his father's guidance, in a family-owned catering business, was where Gabriel Abikzer had his first introduction to the culinary world. Later, he received formal training at the Cordon Bleu. When his cousin, Avi, asked him to join Genadeen Caterers in The Sephardic Temple of Cedarhurst, New York, he seized the opportunity to be the Executive Chef.

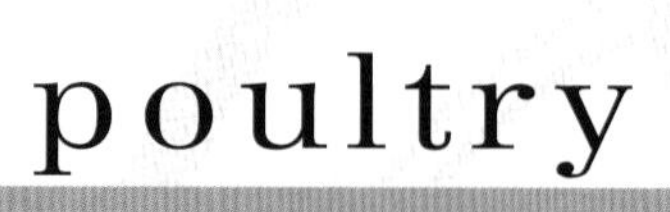
poultry

Oven Roasted Chicken and Haricots Verts

Best Barbequed Chicken

Chicken Roulade

Juicy Roasted Turkey with
Autumn Garnish

Orange Glazed Cornish Hen Stuffed
with Apples

Roasted Duck with Citrus Fruit

Maple Glazed Chicken

Persian Chicken Skewers — Jujeh Kababe

Chicken with Apricots, Cranberries and Dates

Chicken and Dumplings

Oven Roasted Chicken and Haricots Verts

SERVES: 4 | PREP TIME: 10 MINUTES | COOK TIME: 90 MINUTES

- **1 (3 to 4-pound) roasting chicken**
- **2 tablespoons margarine, softened**
- **1 tablespoon each chopped chives, rosemary, thyme, parsley and basil, reserving sprigs for garnish**
- **2 tablespoons chopped garlic**
- **1 orange, halved**
- **2 bay leaves**
- **salt and freshly ground pepper**
- **¼ pound haricots verts or string beans**
- **1 tablespoon mayonnaise**
- **1 tablespoon red wine vinegar**
- **½ teaspoon sugar**

Preheat oven to 350 degrees. With a cleaver or sharp chef's knife, remove end joint from chicken legs and push meat up so that part of bone is exposed. This is known as frenching. In a food processor bowl, mix margarine, chives, rosemary, thyme, parsley, basil and garlic. With your fingers, loosen the skin, freeing it from the chicken meat, without tearing the skin. Spread margarine mixture between skin and chicken meat. Add orange half and bay leaves to cavity of chicken. Squeeze other orange half onto chicken. Season with salt and pepper. Place in pan, breast-side up, and roast 1½ hours.

Bring a pot of salted water to a boil. Add haricots verts and cook 3 minutes. Immediately drain and put into a bowl of ice water. Drain. In small bowl, whisk mayonnaise, vinegar, sugar, salt and pepper. Toss haricot verts with mayonnaise dressing. Carve and slice chicken.

TO PLATE: *On each plate, serve 1 piece of white meat and 1 piece of dark meat. Spoon pan juices over chicken and serve with haricots verts. Garnish with a small bouquet of fresh herbs.*

NOTE: *The original recipe included goat cheese. We have adapted it and it too is fantastic! Tucking herbs under the skin prevents the herbs from burning and allows the flavors to penetrate deep into the chicken meat.*

Haricots verts are thin, elegant French string beans with a sweet flavor. It is easy to overcook them, so avoid walking away while they are blanching.

When purchasing chicken, a broiler is young and tender meat, and is best cooked with high heat, making it the ideal bird to cut up or butterfly for the grill, broiler, sauté pan or frying pan. Braising or stewing a broiler is not a good idea because it tends to dry out. A roaster, on the other hand, has a thick layer of fat, which helps baste the bird as it cooks. It is great for braising, stewing or roasting. A roaster is not good for grilling, broiling or frying, since the outside of the large, thick pieces will overcook, before the inside is cooked through.

From an early age, Chef David Bouley was professionally influenced by his familial French heritage, in particular his grandmother's love for cooking. Bouley was born and raised in Storrs, Connecticut. He honed his skills while working with some of Europe's and America's most acclaimed chefs, eventually earning him four stars from the *New York Times* and James Beard Foundation Awards for: Best Restaurant, Best Chef and Outstanding Chef of the Year. Wherever Chef Bouley goes, he is credited with transporting his clients to unparalleled, new and exciting culinary heights.

Best Barbequed Chicken

SERVES: 6-8 | PREP TIME: 5 MINUTES PLUS OVERNIGHT MARINATING | COOK TIME: 1½ HOURS

2 (2½ to 3-pound) chickens, quartered
1 onion, ¼-inch dice
1 tablespoon minced garlic
¼ cup vegetable oil
½ cup tomato paste
½ cup ketchup
1 cup apple cider vinegar
1 cup honey
½ cup Worcestershire sauce
1 cup Dijon mustard
½ cup soy sauce
1 cup hoisin sauce
2 tablespoons chili powder
1 tablespoon ground cumin
½ tablespoon crushed red pepper flakes
mixed greens

Place chicken pieces into a large glass or plastic container. In a large saucepan on low heat, sauté onions and garlic with oil until onions are translucent, about 4 minutes. Add tomato paste, ketchup, vinegar, honey, Worcestershire sauce, mustard, soy sauce, hoisin sauce, chili powder, cumin and red pepper flakes. Simmer uncovered on low heat for 30 minutes. Pour ⅔ marinade over chicken. Refrigerate both reserved ⅓ marinade and marinated chicken, covered, overnight.

Remove from refrigerator. Preheat oven to 350 degrees. Cook, covered, for ½ hour. Heat a grill. Place chicken quarters on grill, skin side down; cook about 12 minutes. Flip chicken over and grill an additional 10 minutes. The chicken quarters are done when you insert a knife between the leg and the thigh and the juices run clear. Warm reserved sauce and brush over chicken.

TO PLATE: *Serve chicken on a platter, family style. Garnish with mixed greens for color.*

NOTE: *Never use leftover uncooked sauce that raw chicken or meat has been marinating in. The uncooked marinade is a potential breeding ground for food contamination. Instead, use fresh, reserved sauce to brush on cooked chicken or meat.*

In 1978, Ina Garten left her job as a budget analyst in the White House to pursue her dream: operating a specialty food store in Long Island's Hamptons. Shortly after, her title became synonymous with her store's name, Barefoot Contessa. As a celebrity chef, she appears on television, demonstrating recipes from her cookbooks, all of them guaranteed to be tried and true. This barbequed chicken is no exception, given to us by the chef and adapted from The *Barefoot Contessa Cookbook* (Clarkson Potter/Random House 1999).

Chicken Roulade

SERVES: 8 | PREP TIME: 20 MINUTES | COOK TIME: 45 MINUTES

- **8 (6-ounce) boneless dark or white meat chicken cutlets, with skin**
- **2 cups finely chopped dates**
- **½ cup finely chopped pine nuts**
- **½ cup finely chopped pistachios**
- **1 teaspoon ground cardamom**
- **1 teaspoon cayenne pepper**
- **1 teaspoon ground cinnamon**
- **1 teaspoon ground cumin**
- **salt and freshly ground black pepper**
- **2 teaspoons olive oil**
- **¼ teaspoon paprika**
- **parsley sprigs for garnish**

Preheat oven to 375 degrees. Place each of the chicken cutlets, skin-side down, between 2 sheets of plastic wrap. With a meat mallet or the bottom of a frying pan, pound cutlet to ¼-inch thickness.

To prepare stuffing, in a large bowl with a wooden spoon, combine dates, pine nuts, pistachios, cardamom, cayenne pepper, cinnamon and cumin.

To assemble, lightly spray a shallow, glass baking dish with non-stick cooking spray. With cutlet skin-side down, season exposed chicken with salt and pepper, then spread about ¼ cup stuffing over each cutlet. Roll up jelly-roll style. Place chicken, seam-side down, in prepared pan. In a small bowl, combine oil, paprika, salt and pepper. Spread over roulade. Bake 45 minutes. Remove and allow to rest for 10 minutes. Slice with a sharp knife or an electric knife, into 1-inch pinwheels.

TO PLATE: *Fan roulade on a plate and garnish with parsley.*

NOTE: *Roulade, in this case prepared with chicken cutlets, is stuffed and rolled. When sliced, an attractive presentation becomes the focal point — but don't underestimate the taste. Its versatility in allowing for various stuffing choices makes it most appealing.*

Gil Marks, a leading authority on Jewish cuisine, is the author of James Beard Award-winning *Olive Trees and Honey: A Treasury of Vegetarian Recipes from Jewish Communities Around the World, The World of Jewish Desserts, The World of Jewish Entertaining* and James Beard Award finalist, *The World of Jewish Cooking.* He is also an editor and contributing writer for *Kosher Gourmet* magazine. Marks continues to write, lecture and perform cooking demonstrations for groups across the country.

Juicy Roasted Turkey with Autumn Garnish

SERVES: 10 | PREP TIME: 30 MINUTES | COOK TIME: 3¾ HOURS

TURKEY

1 (15-pound) turkey, neck and giblets removed

½ cup margarine, softened

1 teaspoon chopped fresh rosemary

2 tablespoons chopped fresh thyme

1 teaspoon chopped fresh sage

2 teaspoons salt

½ teaspoon ground black pepper

2 onions, sliced

GLAZE

1 cup apricot nectar

1 cup apricot preserves

2 tablespoons honey

GARNISH

1 pound red grapes, cut into small bunches

3 large egg whites, beaten lightly with a fork until only slightly frothy

1 cup granulated or superfine sugar

bunches rosemary, sage, thyme

lady apples, sickle pears, kumquats

Preheat oven to 325 degrees. In a small bowl, combine margarine, rosemary, thyme, sage, salt and pepper. Place turkey, which has been patted dry, into a large roasting pan. Spread half of herbed margarine under breast skin by sliding hand under skin to loosen; spread remainder all over outside of turkey. Tie legs together with kitchen twine. Place breast-side down. Surround with onions. Roast in oven 3 hours.

Meanwhile, in a small pot, over medium-low heat, combine apricot nectar, preserves and honey. Simmer for 10 minutes. Pour over turkey and roast an additional ½ hour. Gently flip to other side and roast 15 minutes longer, or until a meat thermometer inserted into thickest part of thigh (without touching bone) registers 180 degrees and the juices run clear. Remove turkey to a carving board and tent with foil. Allow to rest for 20 minutes.

While turkey is cooking, prepare garnish. With a pastry brush, lightly brush small clusters of grapes with egg whites; the fruit should be barely wet from the whites. Place grapes on a jelly roll pan with sugar, and shake pan so grapes get coated with sugar on all sides. Transfer sugar-coated grapes to a cookie sheet and allow to dry at room temperature. Do not cover.

TO PLATE: *Place turkey on a platter surrounded by seasonal items which might include bunches of rosemary, sage, thyme, sugar-frosted grapes, lady apples, sickle pears and kumquats.*

NOTE: *Typically, turkey is roasted breast-side up. By cooking the turkey with the breast-side down, the juices drain down into the breast eliminating the need for basting. This is guaranteed to be the juiciest turkey you have ever enjoyed.*

This recipe and garnish evolved while taking a food styling course at The Culinary Institute of America. Here, the turkey's presentation is so magnificent, that it serves as the table's centerpiece. As for taste, don't worry about what to do with the leftovers because there won't be any!

Orange Glazed Cornish Hen Stuffed with Apples

SERVES: 4 | PREP TIME: 45 MINUTES PLUS OVERNIGHT MARINATING | COOK TIME: 1 HOUR 20 MINUTES

CORNISH HEN AND MARINADE

¼ cup soy sauce
2 tablespoons toasted sesame oil
1 orange for zest and juice
¼ teaspoon onion powder
¼ teaspoon garlic powder
½ teaspoon paprika
4 (1 to 2-pound) Rock Cornish hens, giblets removed

Prepare marinade by mixing soy sauce, oil, orange zest and juice, onion powder, garlic powder and paprika. Place hens in a container with marinade; refrigerate overnight.

STUFFING

2 tablespoons olive oil
½ onion, diced
1 tablespoon brown sugar
2 Granny Smith apples, peeled, cored and cut into ½-inch cubes
1 orange, juiced

Preheat oven to 375 degrees. To prepare stuffing, in large sauté pan, heat oil over medium-high heat. Add onion and brown sugar. Cook until slightly caramelized, about 4 minutes. Add cubed apples and orange juice. Cook until apples are slightly softened, about 4 minutes. Remove from heat. Remove hens from marinade; stuff with apple mixture and tie legs together with kitchen twine to close cavity. Place in baking dish with legs up.

HONEY GLAZE

2 tablespoons honey
1 tablespoon minced garlic
2 sprigs rosemary leaves, chopped
3 sprigs sage leaves, chopped
3 sprigs thyme leaves, chopped

For glaze, in small bowl, combine honey, garlic, rosemary, sage and thyme. Spread glaze over hens. Cover loosely with foil. Roast 1 hour; uncover and continue roasting 20 minutes.

GARNISH

1 **orange**
1 **tablespoon olive oil**
1 **tablespoon brown sugar**
2 **cinnamon sticks, broken in half**
1 **bunch asparagus**
salt and freshly ground black pepper

Prepare garnish by slicing orange into 8 (⅛-inch) slices. From 4 of the slices, cut outside peel in one place then remove orange flesh so that you have 4 strips of peel. Leave remaining 4 whole slices intact. Set aside. In a sauté pan, over medium heat, add oil, brown sugar and cinnamon sticks. After 2 minutes, remove from heat and set aside. Into pot of boiling salted water, add asparagus. Cook 3 minutes; immediately drain and immerse into ice water. Drain and set aside. Cut and discard kitchen twine from hen.

TO PLATE: *Place hen on a plate. Wrap orange peel strip around 3 or 4 asparagus spears and knot; lean against hen. Stick cinnamon into center of orange slice and lean against hen. Spoon pan juices around plate.*

NOTE: *When storing asparagus, keep spears refrigerated, otherwise they lose sugar and flavor and become tough. When purchasing, look for firm stalks with closed tips.*

The flavors, aromas and colors of Tunisia and Paris weaved the tapestry of Chef Aliza Press's childhood. After receiving formal training at Le Cordon Bleu in Paris, France, she settled in Israel where she established her catering company, Epices & Delices.

Roasted Duck with Citrus Fruit

SERVES: 4 | PREP TIME: 15 MINUTES, PLUS OVERNIGHT THAWING AND OVERNIGHT MARINATING | COOK TIME: 2 HOURS

DUCK AND MARINADE

1 (5-pound) duck, wingtips removed, defrosted in refrigerator
3 cups orange juice
2 buds star anise, ground or crushed
1 orange, quartered
freshly ground black pepper

GLAZE

1 cup orange juice
1 lemon, juiced
1 cup white wine
¼ cup honey
2 tablespoons orange preserves
1 tablespoon soy sauce
1 tablespoon chopped ginger
1 star anise

SIDE DISH AND GARNISH

brown rice with cremini mushrooms, carrots, dried cranberries and pecans (see page 204)
1 orange, peeled and segmented
4 star anise

Place duck in a large sealable plastic bag with orange juice and ground star anise. Marinate, refrigerated, overnight. Preheat oven to 450 degrees. Remove duck from marinade, discarding marinade. Prick skin with a fork, without penetrating flesh. Stuff cavity of duck with orange quarters. Place duck on a rack in a roasting pan, breast-side up. If you do not have a rack, create a nesting base from foil. Season duck with pepper. Roast for 1 hour.

Meanwhile, in a saucepan, add orange and lemon juices, wine, honey, preserves, soy sauce, ginger and star anise. Cook over medium heat at a slow boil, until reduced to half, about 25 minutes.

Reduce oven temperature to 400 degrees. Roast until duck is deep golden brown and a meat thermometer registers 180 degrees when inserted into thickest part of thigh, about 30 minutes. Remove pan and allow to cool. Discard accumulated fat. Using poultry shears, cut duck into quarters. Remove and discard carcass and thigh bones from duck meat. Brush duck with glaze. Return to oven and roast for 30 minutes, until skin is crispy.

TO PLATE: *Place duck quarter on a plate. Spoon sauce on top. Serve with brown rice. Garnish with orange segments and 1 star anise.*

NOTE: *This recipe requires forethought because the frozen duck will first need to be thawed in the refrigerator (for food safety reasons). Once defrosted, the duck is then marinated in the refrigerator. Marinating guarantees juicy meat, while roasting at a high temperature results in a crispy, cooked skin.*

Soon after Jose de Meirelles arrived in New York from Portugal, he was employed as a private driver for a family. He stumbled upon his culinary passion by chance, when he tried his hand at preparing meals for the family. This led him to enroll at The French Culinary Institute in New York, which catapulted his career as a professional chef. At Le Marais in New York City, named for the Jewish neighborhood in Paris, Chef Jose consistently attracts a huge crowd of young couples on dates, business clients, tourists and theatre goers with a variety of menu items including his roasted duck with citrus fruit — Canard Rôti aux Agrumes.

Maple Glazed Chicken

SERVES: 4 | PREP TIME: 5 MINUTES | COOK TIME: 55 MINUTES

CHICKEN AND GLAZE

- **1 (3 to 4-pound) whole chicken, rinsed and patted dry**
- **freshly ground black pepper**
- **⅓ cup pure maple syrup (not pancake syrup)**
- **⅓ cup fresh orange juice**
- **2 tablespoons Dijon mustard**
- **2 tablespoons olive oil**
- **1 tablespoon chopped fresh thyme**
- **¼ teaspoon cayenne pepper**
- **1 teaspoon salt, plus more to taste**

GARNISH

- **1 cup potato purée (see page 200)**
- **12 yellow and green pattypan squash, steamed**

Preheat oven to 400 degrees. Set chicken on a cutting board, breast-side down. Using kitchen shears, cut along both sides of the backbone and remove it (the back bone can be frozen to make chicken broth later). Flip chicken over and press down on breasts to flatten. Sprinkle generously with black pepper. Transfer to a baking dish. In a small saucepan, whisk together maple syrup, orange juice, mustard, oil, thyme, cayenne pepper and salt. Simmer over medium heat until thickened, about 5 minutes. Pour mixture evenly over chicken. Roast chicken, basting occasionally with pan juices, until a thermometer inserted in the deepest part of the thigh registers 170-175 degrees, about 50 minutes. If necessary, add water to pan to prevent juices from burning. Allow chicken to rest for a few minutes, then cut into pieces. Season to taste with salt and pepper.

TO PLATE: *Spoon ¼ cup potato purée onto each dish. Lean chicken against potatoes. Serve pattypan alongside. Spoon pan juices over lacquered chicken.*

NOTE: *This super-moist chicken, with its shiny lacquered glaze, is one of the easiest dinners you can make. It is ready to go into the oven in under 10 minutes. The chicken stays super-moist, even when reheated.*

Pattypan squash is noted for its small size (2-3 inches in diameter), round shape and scalloped edges that make it resemble a small toy top. It comes in yellow, green and white varieties and is often used by chefs to add interest to the plate.

Myra Kornfeld, originally a chef at New York's Angelica Kitchen, has authored multiple cookbooks and is a food columnist. She also shares her knowledge as a culinary teacher at The Natural Gourmet Institute for Health and Culinary Arts, the Institute of Culinary Education and in community centers and gourmet culinary stores. She specializes in cooking parties, corporate team building events and private classes. This recipe was selected for us by the chef from *The Healthy Hedonist* (Simon and Schuster 2005).

Persian Chicken Skewers — Jujeh Kababe

SERVES: 6 | PREP TIME: 10 MINUTES PLUS 6 HOURS OR OVERNIGHT MARINATING | COOK TIME: 10 MINUTES

- **1 large onion, quartered**
- **4 cloves garlic**
- **1 tablespoon paprika**
- **1 teaspoon turmeric**
- **2 tablespoons dried oregano**
- **½ teaspoon salt**
- **½ teaspoon ground black pepper**
- **½ cup fresh lemon juice**
- **1 cup olive oil plus extra for brushing**
- **12 boneless, skinless chicken thighs, cut into 1½-inch cubes**
- **lemon wedges for garnish**

Combine onion, garlic, paprika, turmeric, oregano, salt, pepper and lemon juice in a food processor and process until combined. Add oil through feed tube. Place chicken in a container and toss with marinade to coat well. Cover and refrigerate for at least 6 hours or overnight. Soak wooden skewers in water for 30 minutes to prevent them from burning. Preheat grill or broiler. Thread chicken pieces onto wooden skewers. Brush with a little oil. Grill or broil 5-7 minutes on each side or until meat is opaque throughout.

TO PLATE: *Serve skewers on a plate with lemon wedges for garnish.*

NOTE: *This authentic recipe for Jujeh Kababe is mouth-watering with a blend of unique flavors. Boneless chicken thighs rank high on a grill chef's repertoire. They absorb seasonings, cook quickly and are the juiciest part of the chicken. They are, therefore, used in this recipe as opposed to chicken breasts, which tend to dry out. Marinating infuses the chicken with flavor and the lemon juice, with its acidity, also acts as a tenderizer.*

Joyce Goldstein, renowned, prolific cookbook author and food consultant, is also an expert in menu design, recipe development, staff training and kitchen planning. Her career was jump-started as a chef at Chez Panisse in California. For twelve years, she was the chef/owner of Square One in San Francisco. Chef Joyce is a recipient of several James Beard Awards. She is the founding member of Women Chefs and Restaurateurs and serves on the Awards Committee for the James Beard Foundation. This is a version of her recipe which appears in *Back to Square One: Old-World Food in a New-World Kitchen* (William Morrow and Company, Inc.).

Chicken with Apricots, Cranberries and Dates

SERVES: 8 | PREP TIME: 15 MINUTES PLUS OVERNIGHT MARINATING | COOK TIME: 1½ HOURS

½ cup dried apricots
½ cup dried cranberries
½ cup pitted dates
½ cup orange juice
¼ cup lemon juice
⅓ cup red wine vinegar
½ cup white wine
2 tablespoons olive oil
½ cup brown sugar
1 head garlic, peeled and chopped
2 teaspoons minced ginger
2 tablespoons dried oregano
2 tablespoons dried thyme
2 bay leaves
2 (3½-pound) chickens, cut into eighths
salt and freshly ground pepper

In a large bowl, combine apricots, cranberries, dates, orange and lemon juices, vinegar, wine, oil, brown sugar, garlic, ginger, oregano, thyme and bay leaves. Place chicken in large baking dish. Pour fruit mixture over chicken. Cover and marinate in refrigerator overnight.

Remove baking dish from refrigerator. Preheat oven to 350 degrees. Bake 1 hour, then remove dried fruit from pan, reserving fruit. Return chicken to oven and continue to bake for an additional ½ hour. Discard bay leaves. Season with salt and pepper to taste.

TO PLATE: *Spoon pan juices over chicken with cooked fruit.*

NOTE: *Marinades dramatically increase the flavor of food and can act as a tenderizer too. They typically consist of an acidic ingredient like vinegar, lemon juice or wine, which acts as a tenderizing agent, plus oil, which moisturizes and helps distribute the flavors of the spices that are also added.*

This chicken recipe was inspired by our all-time favorite, Chicken Marbella, that appears in Juliee Rosso and Sheila Lukins's *The Silver Palate Cookbook* (Workman Publishing 1982).

Chicken and Dumplings

SERVES: 4 | PREP TIME: 15 MINUTES | COOK TIME: 45 MINUTES

BROTH

- **1 tablespoon canola oil**
- **½ cup coarsely diced onions**
- **1 cup coarsely diced carrots**
- **½ cup coarsely diced celery**
- **1 quart chicken broth**

DUMPLINGS

- **1⅓ cups all purpose flour**
- **½ tablespoon salt**
- **⅛ teaspoon baking powder**
- **½ teaspoon ground black pepper**
- **1 large egg, lightly beaten**
- **5 tablespoons hot chicken broth**
- **1 tablespoon plus 1 teaspoon canola oil**

CHICKEN AND GARNISH

- **3 cups cooked leftover roasted or rotisserie chicken, shredded with fork**
- **1 tablespoon chopped parsley**

Heat oil in a sauce pot over medium heat. Add onions and cook until soft, about 2 minutes. Add carrots and celery. Cook 1 minute more. Add broth and increase to high heat. Once broth comes to a boil, reduce heat to simmer. Cook until vegetables are done, about 4 minutes. Set aside, keeping broth and vegetables warm.

For dumplings, combine flour, salt, baking powder and pepper in a small bowl; mix well. In a separate bowl, blend egg, chicken broth and oil; mix well. Add dry ingredients to egg mixture and stir with a fork until just mixed together. It is important not to over mix dough or it will become tough. Transfer dough to well-floured board. With floured hands, spread dough out as thin as possible. Lightly flour surface of dough and finish rolling to a thickness of ⅛-inch. Return broth and vegetables to stove; simmer over medium heat. Cut dough on the bias into 3 x 1-inch rectangular strips. Tie each strip into a knot and drop into simmering stock, a few at a time. Stir stock to prevent dumplings from sticking together. Cook 6-8 minutes or until dumplings are cooked through and tender. Add chicken and cook 1 minute longer. Turn off heat and let stand 3 minutes before serving.

TO PLATE: *Ladle into shallow soup bowls; garnish with chopped parsley.*

NOTE: *This all-inclusive dish is bound to be one that you will prepare often. It is full of flavor and can be made quickly and easily, making use of leftover or rotisserie chicken.*

Michel Nischan gets rave reviews for the Dressing Room restaurant located in a rustic-chic farmhouse in Westport, Connecticut, which he co-owns with Paul Newman. Nischan is a James Beard award-winning, best-selling author and a very creative chef. Through his advocacy for an enhanced, healthful, organic and sustainable planet, Nischan met Newman. In keeping with their mutually altruistic natures, the owners donate a portion of Dressing Room's proceeds to worthy causes. The chef is publicly recognized for creating a cuisine of "well-being, focused on respect for pure, local, organic ingredients and their intense flavors — without the use of highly processed, overly indulgent ingredients." This chef concentrates on American heirloom recipes that represent the best of New England.

fish

Crisp Paupiette of Halibut in a Potato Crust

Seared Sea Bass with Grilled Pineapple Rice
Encircled by Baby Bok Choy

Glazed Salmon in Mirin

Stuffed Salmon Florentine

Chilean Sea Bass with
Risotto, Wild Mushrooms and Peas

Cajun Blackened Salmon with
Spicy Grilled Corn, Black Beans and
Roasted Red Pepper Salad

Miso Marinated Sea Bass

Grilled Tuna with Citrus Salsa

Flounder with Beets and Sugar Snap Peas

Italian Mediterranean Sea Bass with Potatoes

Pan-Seared Tuna with Wasabi Cream Sauce

Crisp Paupiette of Halibut in a Potato Crust

SERVES: 4 | PREP TIME: 10 MINUTES | COOK TIME: 15 MINUTES

HALIBUT AND POTATO

4 (4-ounce) portions skinless halibut filet
salt and freshly ground black pepper
4 sprigs fresh thyme, leaves only, chopped, reserve some for garnish
4 baby red potatoes, peeled
1 egg yolk, lightly beaten
2 tablespoons olive oil

SPINACH AND LEEKS

2 tablespoons olive oil, divided
2 leeks, white part only, thinly sliced
2 pounds fresh spinach
salt and freshly ground black pepper

GARNISH

1 lemon, halved
1 tablespoon minced chives

Dry halibut well with a paper towel. Season with salt and pepper and sprinkle with chopped thyme. Using a vegetable slicer or mandoline, slice each potato into very thin rounds, about 1⁄16-inch thick. Do not rinse potato slices, as their starch will help slices stick together. Brush halibut with some of the egg yolk. Arrange potato slices overlapping on fillet so that potato looks like fish scales covering entire top of the fish. Brush top of potatoes with remaining egg yolk.

To prepare leeks, heat 1 tablespoon oil in a sauté pan. Over medium heat, add leeks and cook until soft, about 4 minutes. Remove leeks. In same sauté pan, heat remaining 1 tablespoon oil. Add spinach and sauté over low heat until wilted, about 1 minute. Combine leeks and spinach together. Season to taste with salt and pepper. Keep warm.

Heat 2 tablespoons oil in a large pan over medium heat. Season potato-side of halibut with salt and pepper and fry potato-side down until golden brown, about 3 minutes. Carefully turn and cook an additional 5 minutes.

TO PLATE: *Place bed of spinach-leek mixture onto warm plate. Lean paupiette of halibut, potato crust side up, against spinach-leek mixture. Squeeze with lemon. Garnish fish with reserved thyme leaves. Sprinkle outer edge of plate with minced chives.*

NOTE: *With their multi-layers, leeks provide nooks for hidden dirt and sand. The best way to clean them is to chop them, then soak in a bowl of water. Rather than pouring the leeks and water through a strainer, which would put the sand back onto the leeks, lift the leeks out of the water with your hands. Discard water and sand that has been left behind. Repeat until no sand is deposited on the bottom of the bowl.*

To remove thyme leaves from the stem, run pinched fingertips down the stem from the top and the leaves will fall off.

In many of the recipes, we make use of a mandoline which is a most worthwhile utensil that is frequently used in professional kitchens to make slices even in thickness. This is important for uniformity in cooking time, as well as for presentation. Another advantage is that foods can be sliced very thin, with less effort than would be required with a knife. This is a dangerous utensil because of the sharpness of the blade. It can, however, be used without fear of injury by wearing a cut resistant glove. Both can be purchased in a kitchen supply store.

Daniel Boulud is the chef/owner of five award-winning restaurants and the author of six cookbooks. While he comes from Lyon and trained under France's most renowned chefs, he continues to master the culinary scene in New York. His accolades include the James Beard Foundation awards for Outstanding Restaurateur, Best Chef of New York City and Outstanding Chef of the Year. In addition to being the recipient of awards given by *Gourmet Magazine, The New York Times* and *Zagat,* his restaurant, Daniel, has been named "one of the ten best restaurants in the world" by the *International Herald Tribune*. This recipe, originally prepared with sea bass, has been adapted from *Cooking With Daniel Boulud* (Random House).

Seared Sea Bass with Grilled Pineapple Rice Encircled by Baby Bok Choy

SERVES: 4 | PREP TIME: 15 MINUTES | COOK TIME: 40 MINUTES

PINEAPPLE RICE

- ¼ cup rum
- 1 tablespoon butter or margarine
- 1 tablespoon light brown sugar
- ½ ripe pineapple, peeled and cut into ¼-inch thick rounds
- 1 cup basmati rice
- 2 tablespoons canola oil
- ¼ small onion, finely diced
- 1 teaspoon minced garlic
- ½ red bell pepper, ¼-inch dice
- ½ zucchini, ¼-inch dice
- 2 tablespoons mixed chopped cilantro and scallions
- salt and freshly ground black pepper

In a sauté pan, combine rum, butter and sugar; simmer over low heat until sugar is melted, about 4 minutes. Heat grill pan to high. Brush this glaze mixture on each side of pineapple slices and grill until browned, 2-3 minutes on each side. Cut into ¼-inch diced pieces. Follow directions on package to cook rice. Meanwhile, in a clean sauté pan over medium-high heat, add oil, onion and garlic. Sauté 2 minutes. Add diced pineapple, red bell pepper, zucchini and cilantro and scallions. Sauté 2 minutes. Remove; combine together with cooked rice, salt and pepper in a bowl.

GARNISH

- 1 tablespoon canola oil
- ½ zucchini, julienne
- ½ red bell pepper, julienne
- ½ yellow bell pepper, julienne

For garnish, using same sauté pan, heat oil. Add zucchini and red and yellow bell peppers. Sauté on medium-high heat for 2 minutes. Remove from heat, set aside.

BABY BOK CHOY

- 4 baby bok choy, bottoms trimmed but left intact, sliced in half lengthwise
- salt

Cook bok choy in boiling, salted water for 4 minutes. Immediately immerse bok choy in ice cold water to stop the cooking process and to retain the vibrant green color. Drain. Season to taste with salt.

GARLIC GINGER SAUCE

½ cup soy sauce
2 tablespoons rice wine vinegar or lime juice
½ teaspoon toasted sesame oil
½ cup sugar
1 teaspoon minced garlic
1 teaspoon minced ginger

Take fish out of the refrigerator 15 minutes before cooking to bring it to room temperature. Make sauce by mixing soy sauce, vinegar, oil and sugar in a small sauce pot. Bring to a boil. Add garlic and ginger. Reduce heat and simmer 10 minutes. Strain, using fine mesh strainer, reserving liquid.

FISH

4 (5½-ounce) sea bass fillets with skin
salt and freshly ground black pepper
2 tablespoons canola oil

Season fish with salt and pepper on both sides. Heat a large sauté pan over high heat for 2 minutes. Pour oil into pan and wait 1 minute. Carefully lay fish in pan, skin-side down, and cook until skin is crisp, about 3-4 minutes. Turn fish over, lower heat to medium-low and cook 3 more minutes. Remember that fish continues to cook once you remove it. When ready to plate, warm components.

TO PLATE: *Spray a 3½-inch round mold or a can with top and bottom removed, with non-stick cooking spray. Place onto center of plate. With a spoon, pack rice into mold. Remove mold. Wrap baby bok choy around rice. Top with fish and garnish with julienne vegetables. Spoon sauce on plate.*

NOTE: *The acid and sweetness of the fruit perfectly balance the richness of the sea bass, making it a delicious combination. As for presentation, if this dish were served to you in the best restaurant, you would be impressed!*

While we were on vacation at the Mauna Lani Hotel in Kona, Hawaii, a guest who had been employed by Honolulu's award-winning chef, Alan Wong, shared this great recipe.

Glazed Salmon in Mirin

SERVES: 4 | PREP TIME: 5 MINUTES PLUS 1 HOUR OR OVERNIGHT MARINATING | COOK TIME: 2 MINUTES

SALMON

4 (6-ounce, 1-inch thick) salmon steaks

MARINADE

1½ tablespoons mirin

1 tablespoon soy sauce

1 teaspoon brown sugar

1 teaspoon red hot pepper sauce

LEMON DRESSING

2 tablespoons extra virgin olive oil

1 tablespoon fresh lemon juice

1 teaspoon dark sesame oil

¼ teaspoon salt

¼ teaspoon red hot pepper sauce

RICE

1 cup cooked white rice

GARNISH

2 teaspoons sesame seeds, toasted in a non-stick skillet

8 chives

Place salmon in a plastic sealable bag. To prepare marinade, in a bowl, combine mirin, soy sauce, sugar and pepper sauce. Pour marinade into bag and marinate in refrigerator for at least 1 hour or overnight.

When ready to cook, whisk oil, lemon juice, sesame oil, salt and pepper sauce in a small bowl. Set aside.

Heat a large non-stick skillet until hot. Remove salmon steaks from marinade and arrange them in hot skillet. Cover and cook over medium-high heat for about 2 minutes, or until bottoms of salmon steaks are nicely browned and tops are cooked through from steam created in covered pan. The salmon should be slightly rare in center.

TO PLATE: *Place salmon on a plate. Fill empty space in center of salmon steak with ¼ cup rice. Drizzle lemon dressing over salmon steaks and sprinkle with toasted sesame seeds. Garnish with chives.*

NOTE: *Mirin, an essential condiment in Japanese cuisine, is a rice wine similar to sake, but with a lower alcohol content. The marinade gives the salmon a sweet, nutty flavor and a beautiful color, while the lemon dressing provides a good contrast to the sweetness of the fish. Although marinating is preferred, if you are pressed for time, you can cook the fish right away.*

Jacques Pepin is one of America's best-known chefs, cooking instructors and food writers. Formally trained at the Grand Hotel de l'Europe and at the Plaza Athénée in Paris, he later served as personal chef to three French heads of state, including Charles de Gaulle. In addition to his culinary expertise, he holds a masters degree in French Literature from Columbia University. He has written 24 books and has hosted numerous public television series, including the award winning "Julia and Jacques Cooking at Home" in which he shared the spotlight with Julia Child. He also received France's highest civilian honor, the French Legion of Honor. He is Dean at the French Culinary Institute in New York. This recipe can also be found in *Jacques Pepin: Fast Food My Way* (Houghton Mifflin Company).

Stuffed Salmon Florentine

SERVES: 8 | PREP TIME: 15 MINUTES | COOK TIME: 15 MINUTES

1 tablespoon olive oil, divided
10 ounces button mushrooms, sliced
7 ounces baby spinach
1 tablespoon minced garlic, divided
¼ cup breadcrumbs
1 egg
1 teaspoon garlic powder
2 pounds whole salmon fillet (ask fish monger to skin and butterfly)
¼ teaspoon salt
¼ teaspoon paprika
¼ cup vegetable or parve chicken broth
1 lemon for garnish
1 lime for garnish
8 small sprigs parsley for garnish

Heat a large skillet with 1 teaspoon oil. Add mushrooms and sauté for 3 minutes. Add spinach; cook until spinach is wilted, but still a bright green, about 30 seconds. Add 1 teaspoon minced garlic. Empty contents of pan into a bowl. To this, add breadcrumbs, egg and garlic powder. Mix with a wooden spoon. Lay fish out flat. Spread a thin layer of spinach mixture over exposed surface of fish. Roll fish tightly to form a long log. Using 8 pieces of kitchen twine, tie each piece around log 1 inch apart. Place log into a rectangular baking dish. Refrigerate fish for 15 minutes. In a small bowl, make a paste of remaining 2 teaspoons oil, remaining 2 teaspoons garlic, salt and paprika.

Preheat oven to 350 degrees. On a cutting board, with a very sharp knife, cut salmon log into 8 spiral pieces in between the twine. Lay each spiral on its side in a baking dish. Spread ¼ teaspoon paste over each spiral. Pour broth into dish. Bake 10 minutes. When cool enough to handle, remove twine.

For garnish, slice lemons and limes thinly. Make a cut from center to peel. Layer 1 lemon slice and 1 lime. Hold slices in fingers of both hands, with fingers on each side of cut. Twist in opposite directions. Top with parsley sprig.

TO PLATE: *Serve salmon spiral on plate with lemon-lime twist.*

Manuel Suquilema, an enthusiastic and innovative fish monger, is always experimenting. This collaborative recipe between Manuel and one of the local private chefs, is aesthetically attractive. Best of all, no one will be the wiser as to how easy it is to prepare.

Chilean Sea Bass with Risotto, Wild Mushrooms and Peas

SERVES: 4 | PREP TIME: 15 MINUTES | COOK TIME: 1 HOUR

MUSHROOMS

14 ounces mixed wild mushrooms
½ lemon, juiced
2 cloves garlic, mashed
2 thyme sprigs, leaves only
2 tablespoons olive oil
salt and freshly ground black pepper

Preheat oven to 250 degrees. Place mushrooms in a baking dish with lemon juice, garlic, thyme, oil, salt and pepper. Bake 20 minutes. When cool enough to handle, dice half of mushrooms for risotto and slice remaining half for garnish. Set aside.

PEAS

1 tablespoon butter
1 cup peas (from 1 pound in pod or, if unavailable, substitute frozen)
salt
⅓ cup water
2 ounces pea shoots

Heat sauté pan over medium heat for 1 minute. Add butter; when melted add peas. Reduce heat to low and sauté gently, shaking the pan every so often for 3 minutes. Season with salt. Add water; increase heat to medium. Cook 1 minute. Turn off heat and toss in pea shoots.

RISOTTO

2 tablespoons olive oil
1 shallot, finely chopped
1 clove garlic, finely chopped
1 cup risotto
½ cup white wine
3-4 cups hot vegetable or parve chicken flavored broth
2 tablespoons butter
2 tablespoons grated Parmesan cheese
chopped chives for garnish
salt and freshly ground black pepper

In a large pan, over medium heat, add oil and sauté shallot, garlic and risotto for 4 minutes. Add wine and cook until liquid is absorbed, stirring with a wooden spoon. Add hot broth, one ladle at a time, stirring continuously and waiting until liquid is absorbed before adding more; this will take about 20 minutes. Add diced mushrooms to risotto. Let risotto rest for 1-2 minutes. Stir in butter and Parmesan cheese. Add chopped chives. Season with salt and pepper to taste.

CHILEAN SEA BASS

4 (6-ounce) Chilean sea bass fillets, with skin
salt and freshly ground black pepper
2 tablespoons canola oil

Remove fish from refrigerator 15 minutes before cooking, allowing it to reach room temperature. Heat a large sauté pan over high heat for 2 minutes. Season fish with salt and pepper, flesh side only. Pour oil into pan and wait 1 minute. Carefully lay fish in pan, skin-side down, and cook for 3-4 minutes, until skin is crisp. Turn fish over, lower heat to medium-low and cook for 3 more minutes.

When ready to serve, warm components of recipe.

TO PLATE: *Spoon risotto into a pyramid mold and turn onto center of plate. Remove mold. Lean sea bass against risotto, and surround with sliced mushrooms. Spoon peas and pea shoots on top.*

NOTE: *Pea shoots are the young leaves and tendrils of pea plants. Pea shoots have a distinct, light pea flavor with a hint of sweetness. Pea shoots can be stored covered with a paper towel in the refrigerator for 1-2 days.*

Risotto is a creamy rice dish in which broth is stirred into a short-grain or Arborio rice that has been sautéed. It demands a watchful eye and an active hand as it cooks. Liquid is added in small batches, while stirring. Each batch of liquid needs to be absorbed before the next is added. At this point the risotto should be al dente. Once the butter and Parmesan cheese are stirred in, the final result is neither soupy nor dry, but a perfect creamy, sauce-coated risotto.

How does a chef know when fish is cooked enough? First, a metal skewer inserted into the fish for 5 seconds should go in easily and the skewer should feel hot when touched to your lip. Another method, similar to testing meat, is to feel the fish with your fingers. The fish should feel like the soft part of your hand between your thumb and index finger when you form a loose fist.

Zorko-Zoran Glavan, originally from Croatia, began his culinary career as a chef on a popular cruise line which eventually landed him a job as a sous-chef for entertainer Frank Sinatra. In recent years, he has won several awards during his tenure position as Executive Chef at Frank's Waterside in New Jersey.

Cajun Blackened Salmon with Spicy Grilled Corn, Black Beans and Roasted Red Pepper Salad

SERVES: 4 | PREP TIME: 8 MINUTES | COOK TIME: 20 MINUTES

GRILLED CORN SALAD

4 ears fresh corn, husked
2 red bell peppers
1 (15-ounce) can black beans, rinsed and drained
½ cup chopped cilantro
½ jalapeño pepper, seeds and membranes removed, ⅛-inch dice
½ cup extra virgin olive oil
2 limes, juiced
salt

BLACKENING SPICE

2 tablespoons kosher salt
5 tablespoons paprika
1 tablespoon dried thyme
1 tablespoon ground black pepper
1 tablespoon garlic powder
½ teaspoon cayenne pepper
½ teaspoon ground white pepper

SALMON

4 (6-ounce) skinless salmon fillets
4 tablespoons canola oil

On a well-oiled grill, cook corn until lightly charred, about 3 minutes. When cool enough to handle, cut kernels from cob. Grill whole red bell peppers until black on all sides, about 10 minutes. Place red bell peppers in a bowl; cover with plastic wrap. After 10 minutes, remove blackened skin, stems and seeds. Cut red bell peppers into strips. In bowl, combine corn, red bell peppers, black beans, cilantro, jalapeño, oil and lime juice. Season with salt. Set aside.

In a small bowl, combine salt, paprika, thyme, black pepper, garlic powder, cayenne and white pepper. Coat salmon well on both sides with blackening spice. Heat oil in a large, heavy sauté pan or cast iron skillet until almost smoking. Add salmon and sear for about 2 minutes; flip to other side and cook an additional 2 minutes.

TO PLATE: *Place grilled corn salad in center of plate; top with blackened salmon.*

The Aussie Gourmet is the perfect name for chef/owner Naomi Nachman's catering business. Originally from Australia with a passion for food, Naomi is also the founder of the Kosher Culinary Institute on Long Island, where she teaches recreational cooking to adults and is the representative chef for Ossie's Fish of Brooklyn, New York.

Miso Marinated Sea Bass

SERVES: 4 | PREP TIME: 10 MINUTES PLUS OVERNIGHT MARINATING | COOK TIME: 40 MINUTES

MARINADE

1 cup orange juice

1 cup brown sugar

1 cup white wine or sake

1½ tablespoons chili sauce

¼ cup white miso paste

4 (6-ounce) skinless sea bass fillets

PASTA

1 (8-ounce) package angel hair pasta

3 tablespoons sesame oil

3 tablespoons soy sauce

3 tablespoons orange juice

MANGO, GRAPEFRUIT, POMEGRANATE RELISH

1 mango, pitted, peeled, small dice

1 pink grapefruit, peeled and sectioned

½ cup pomegranate seeds or dried cranberries

In a saucepan, combine orange juice, sugar, wine or sake, chili sauce and miso. Bring to a boil. Remove and allow to cool. Pour over fish; cover and refrigerate overnight. Remove fish from marinade. Preheat broiler. Put fish in a baking dish and broil until top is golden brown, about 5 minutes. Watch carefully to avoid burning. Decrease oven to 350 degrees and bake 30 minutes. Meanwhile, cook pasta al dente, according to directions on box. Drain and toss with oil, soy sauce and orange juice.

Prepare relish by gently tossing mango, grapefruit and pomegranate seeds or dried cranberries together.

TO PLATE: *Place fish on a bed of pasta; garnish with mango, grapefruit and pomegranate relish.*

NOTE: *Miso, a traditional Japanese rich, thick and salty paste is made from fermented soybeans, barley, rice or other grains. There are different varieties of miso. In general, the darker the color, the stronger the taste.*

The only edible part of the pomegranate is the seeds. To dislodge and collect the seeds, cut the fruit horizontally at the equator. Hold the fruit, cut-side down, over a bowl and hit the back of the pomegranate with a wooden spoon.

Bruce Soffer, previously the exclusive caterer for the New York Academy of Sciences, is a graduate of the French Culinary Institute. He offers his culinary services in creating the most glamorous home dinner parties, detail oriented on-site corporate events and the most spectacular gala affairs at the venue of your choice. His expertise has earned him rave reviews.

Grilled Tuna with Citrus Salsa

SERVES: 4 | PREP TIME: 30 MINUTES | COOK TIME: 15 MINUTES

CITRUS SALSA

1 medium lemon, zest removed and minced
1 medium lime
1 medium orange
1 medium-size pink grapefruit
1 tangerine or Clementine
¾ cup light corn syrup
½ cup white vinegar
½ cup orange juice
1 jalapeño pepper, seeded, small dice
1 red bell pepper, small dice
½ red onion, small dice
½ bunch scallions, sliced thin
2 tablespoons chopped fresh cilantro
salt and freshly ground black pepper
4 sprigs cilantro for garnish

Remove sections from lemon, lime, orange, grapefruit and tangerine. Set aside. In a small saucepan, combine corn syrup, vinegar and orange juice. Cook until this gastrique is reduced by three-quarters. Add lemon zest and jalapeño. Allow to cool, then combine with sectioned fruit, red bell pepper, onion, scallions, cilantro, salt and pepper.

FISH

1 tablespoon salt
1 teaspoon ground black pepper
1 tablespoon garlic powder
1 teaspoon dried thyme
1 teaspoon dried basil
1 teaspoon dried oregano
1 tablespoon paprika
1 teaspoon onion powder
4 (6-ounce) tuna steaks
2 teaspoons oil

In a small bowl, combine salt, pepper, garlic powder, thyme, basil, oregano, paprika and onion powder. Dust tuna with this mixture. Heat grill pan until very hot. Add oil, then tuna; cook 2 minutes. Turn fish to other side for 2 additional minutes.

TO PLATE: *Center tuna steak on dinner plate. Spoon a portion of citrus salsa over top. Garnish with cilantro sprig.*

NOTE: *In a professional kitchen, peeling citrus fruits and separating the segments (referred to as supremes) is performed with ease. With a sharp chef's knife, slice the two ends of the orange off, just to the point of exposing the pulp of the fruit and flattening the ends. Then stand the orange up, with one of the cut ends on the cutting board. Cutting in strips from top to bottom, place the knife between the pith and the pulp and begin to cut downward, following the contour of the fruit so you only remove the pith and membrane, and not the pulp. Repeat until orange is peeled. To section, working over a bowl, using a paring knife, cut between the membranes, releasing the segments and allowing them and their juices to collect in a bowl. When you finish each fruit, squeeze the remaining juice from the membranes into the bowl, discarding the membranes. The collected juice can be used instead of plain orange juice for the gastrique. A gastrique is a thick sauce that is made by reducing vinegar or wine, sugar or corn syrup and usually fruit juice.*

As the executive chef at the famed Commander's Palace restaurant in New Orleans, 30-year old Tory McPhail had big clogs to fill, following in the footsteps of household names like Emeril Lagasse. In his first year at the helm, he was a James Beard Rising Star Chef Nominee. Tory McPhail continues to make his mark at Commander's.

Flounder with Beets and Sugar Snap Peas

SERVES: 4 | PREP TIME: 10 MINUTES | COOK TIME: 1 HOUR 10 MINUTES

1 pound beets, scrubbed and dried
½ cup extra virgin olive oil, plus more for drizzling
sea salt and freshly ground black pepper
½ cup packed mint leaves, chop half
1¼ cups seasoned panko or breadcrumbs
½ cup instant blending flour (for example, Wondra)
½ teaspoon salt
½ teaspoon ground black pepper
3 large eggs
4 (5-ounce) flounder fillets, halved lengthwise
1 pound sugar snap peas
¼ cup canola oil
3 tablespoons unsalted butter

Preheat oven to 350 degrees. Place each beet on a square of aluminum foil. Drizzle with oil to lightly coat and season with a sprinkling of salt and pepper. Wrap loosely in foil. Place packets on a jelly roll pan and then in oven. Roast until beets are easily pierced with the point of a knife, about 1 hour. Remove from oven and cool. When cool enough to handle, wearing rubber gloves to prevent staining, rub each beet with paper towel to remove skin. Cut beets into ½-inch dice pieces. Set aside.

In a shallow bowl, combine half of mint leaves that have been chopped with breadcrumbs. In another shallow bowl, season flour with salt and pepper. In third bowl, lightly beat eggs. Dredge each flounder fillet in seasoned flour, then dip in beaten egg, then in breadcrumbs. Set aside on a jelly roll pan. In a large sauté pan, heat ½ cup olive oil. Add sugar snap peas and sauté for 1 minute. Season with salt. Add diced beets and remaining mint and continue cooking for 1 minute. Remove from heat. In another large, preferably non-stick, sauté pan, heat canola oil until hot but not smoking. Add butter. When foam subsides, add fillets; you should hear them sizzle. Cook until golden brown, about 3-4 minutes per side. Transfer cooked fillets to a paper towel-lined platter and season immediately with salt and pepper.

TO PLATE: *Lay 2 fillet halves parallel to each other. On a third parallel line criss-cross sugar snap peas. Spoon beets in between snap peas.*

NOTE: *Buy beets with their tops still attached, which is an indication of their freshness. The beets, providing an earthy, just sweet enough touch, can be made a day in advance.*

When using flour for gravy, batter or breading, some chefs prefer to use instant blending flour, a low protein flour that has been formulated to dissolve quickly in both hot and cold liquids and is less likely to form clumps.

David Pasternack is the chef/partner (along with Mario Batali and Joseph Bastianich) of seafood mecca, Esca, in New York City. Aside from having worked at other top-flight restaurants, he, along with Ed Levine, is the co-author of *The Young Man & the Sea* (Workman Publishing), from which the chef has selected this recipe for us.

Italian Mediterranean Sea Bass with Potatoes

SERVES: 4 | PREP TIME: 15 MINUTES | COOK TIME: 45 MINUTES

MARINADE

½ cup extra virgin olive oil

¼ cup white wine vinegar

1 tablespoon chopped rosemary

salt and freshly ground black pepper

FISH, POTATOES AND OLIVES

2 pounds peeled Yukon Gold potatoes, sliced ¼-inch thin

4 (6-ounce) sea bass fillets

½ cup kalamata, Niçoise or any other Italian olive, pitted

½ cup grape tomatoes, halved

GARNISH

4 rosemary sprigs

Preheat oven to 400 degrees. In a small bowl, whisk oil, vinegar, rosemary, salt and pepper. Divide marinade in half.

Rinse potato slices in cold water, drain and dry. In a bowl, combine potatoes with half of marinade. Spread potato slices out completely covering bottom of an oven-proof dish. Bake 25 minutes. Top potatoes with fish. Pour remaining marinade over fish. Add olives and tomatoes; bake an additional 20 minutes.

TO PLATE: *Lift the fillets onto a warm plate. Lay potatoes alongside fish and pour the pan juices, olives and tomatoes over fish. Spear each fillet with a rosemary sprig.*

NOTE: *The chef suggests using kalamata olives, either dry-cured or oil-cured, rather than those cured in brine. Unlike the brine-cured, in which much of the olive's flavor is lost, dry-curing and oil-curing removes much of the olive's bitterness while retaining all of the rich, pure, olive flavor.*

There is something very reassuring about a restaurant with an open kitchen. The unspoken message is that there is nothing to hide. On the contrary, this form of preparation provides an entertaining showcase. Tides, located in New York City, is known for its fabulous fresh fish, where quality is never compromised. It is home to talented Executive Chef and co-owner Judy Seto, whose recipe served as the inspiration for this dish.

Pan-Seared Tuna with Wasabi Cream Sauce

SERVES: 6 | PREP TIME: 10 MINUTES | COOK TIME: 25 MINUTES

AVOCADO SAUCE

1 avocado, peeled and pitted

1 tablespoon olive oil

1 tablespoon fresh lemon juice

¼ cup water plus up to ¼ cup more to reach desired consistency

salt and freshly ground black pepper

TUNA

6 (4-ounce) portions sushi grade tuna

½ cup maple syrup

½ cup soy sauce

¼ cup wasabi powder

3 tablespoons water

¼ cup sesame seeds

2 tablespoons olive oil

GARNISH

1 yellow squash

1 zucchini

1 tablespoon olive oil

2 tablespoons chili sauce

Returning from a restaurant, raving about this dish, we couldn't wait to roll up our sleeves and recreate this recipe. It is guaranteed to receive a standing ovation. We are indebted to Wolfgang Puck of Spago for his plating creativity.

To prepare avocado sauce, put avocado, oil, lemon juice and water into a blender or a food processor. Purée until smooth. Add more water, a little bit at a time, until consistency is a creamy liquid. Season with salt and pepper to taste. Set aside.

To prepare tuna, place each portion individually in plastic wrap. With hands, roll fish to form a log or rectangular shape that is 1¼ inches thick; refrigerate. Meanwhile, in a small saucepan, combine maple syrup and soy sauce. Over medium-high heat, cook until sauce is reduced to half, about 20 minutes. Then in a small bowl, mix wasabi powder with water. Place sesame seeds on a plate. Unwrap tuna and spread with wasabi; press sesame seeds on both sides of tuna. Heat oil in a skillet over medium-high heat until very hot, almost to smoking. Gently put tuna into pan and sear for 20 seconds on each side, using a spatula to turn. Remove from pan. Allow to rest.

Using a vegetable peeler, cut squash and zucchini into long, wide strips. Discard core (including seeds). Heat oil in a skillet over medium-high heat. Add squash and zucchini; sauté, stirring often until bright in color, about 3 minutes. Season to taste with salt and pepper.

On a cutting board, with a sharp knife or an electric knife, cut tuna into ½-inch slices. Place chili sauce into a squirt bottle.

TO PLATE: *The plating of this dish will depend on the shape of your plate. If you have a round plate, place cooked squash ribbons in the center. Arrange fish around squash. Spoon avocado sauce around outside of plate. In the center of sauce, squeeze design of chili sauce. Drizzle maple soy sauce on top of tuna. If your plate is elliptical, try plating as we have done in the photograph.*

dairy

Eggplant, Sun-Dried Tomatoes
and Goat Cheese Rollatini

Braided Bread Filled with
Pesto, Dried Tomatoes, Cheese and Olives

Wheat Berry and Barley
with Mozzarella Cheese

Scalloped Potatoes

Greek Salad Pizza

Home-Made Manicotti with
Ricotta Cheese and Tomato Sauce

Eggplant, Sun-Dried Tomatoes and Goat Cheese Rollatini

SERVES: 4 | PREP TIME: 30 MINUTES | COOK TIME: 8 HOURS

16 plum tomatoes

¼ cup extra virgin olive oil

4 cloves garlic, lightly smashed with side of knife blade

1 bunch basil leaves

2 (½-pound) firm eggplants

olive oil

kosher salt

4 ounces soft goat cheese, cut into 12 slices

fleur de sel (optional)

Preheat oven to 250 degrees. Cut plum tomatoes in half, lengthwise. Remove core root by cutting a small triangle at the base and discarding. Place cut side up onto an ungreased jelly roll pan. Roast 6-8 hours. When cool, layer tomatoes in a jar with oil, garlic and 6 basil leaves; tomatoes must be submerged in oil.

Preheat oven to broil. Slice eggplants lengthwise with a mandoline or knife into ¼-inch slices. Arrange in a single layer on a greased jelly roll pan. Brush eggplant slices with oil and sprinkle with salt. Broil 6 minutes; carefully turn with spatula and broil an additional 4 minutes. Remove tomatoes from oil. With hands, peel and discard skin on tomatoes. To assemble, top each eggplant slice with 2 tomato halves, 1 goat cheese slice and 1 basil leaf at the bottom of the narrow end of the eggplant. Roll, beginning at the end with the filling; place seam-side down into a flat container until ready to serve.

TO PLATE: *Place 2 sun-dried tomato halves onto plate. Put basil sprig on top of tomatoes. Lay 3 rollatini, seam-side down, with end-point facing in. Drizzle with olive oil. Sprinkle with fleur de sel or kosher salt. Serve at room temperature.*

NOTE: *You can roast extra tomatoes and store them in an airtight container in the refrigerator, as long as the tomatoes are submerged in oil. The oil acts as a preservative, extending the shelf life. Serve tomatoes on toasted Italian bread, or use as an ingredient when making fish or pasta.*

The key role of salt is to enhance flavor. Many chefs use different types of salt at different stages of the cooking process. Kosher salt, with its cube-like structure, is used while cooking because it dissolves rapidly when added to water or sauces. For finishing dishes, chefs rely on sea salt, which is less salty than table salt. It has a distinctive, natural, mineral flavor. Fleur de sel, the most expensive of the choices, is a coarse-grain sea salt that is obtained by hand-harvesting crystals that form on the surface of salt ponds. It has a light, crunchy texture and is best used by sprinkling onto foods just before serving. Chefs avoid table salt because of the iodine and anti-caking ingredients, which can impart a chemical taste.

Home hospitality takes on a whole new dimension when you are welcomed by Chef Ronen and Genine Bar-El of Bar-El Catering. When they serve you their mouth-watering gourmet vegetarian cuisine in a 150-year old historic house nestled in the unique atmosphere of Safed, Israel, a culinary memory is sure to be made and treasured.

Braided Bread Filled with Pesto, Dried Tomatoes, Cheese and Olives

SERVES: 8 | PREP TIME: 20 MINUTES | COOK TIME: 25 MINUTES

1 purchased pizza dough or prepare dough according to recipe

DOUGH

1 tablespoon active dry yeast

1 cup warm water, divided

1 teaspoon plus 3 tablespoons sugar, divided

3 tablespoons olive oil

2¾ cups all purpose flour

1 teaspoon salt

FILLING

3 tablespoons purchased pesto

3 tablespoons finely chopped sun-dried tomatoes, packed in oil

1 cup shredded mozzarella cheese

½ cup grated Parmesan cheese

⅓ cup sliced green olives

EGG WASH

1 egg

1 tablespoon water

To prepare dough, mix yeast with ½ cup warm water. Add 1 teaspoon sugar. Set aside for 10 minutes. Add oil. In a food processor, pulse flour, salt and remaining 3 tablespoons sugar for three seconds. Add yeast mixture and remaining ½ cup warm water. Pulse 5 seconds or until dough forms a ball. If dough is sticky, add up to 2 tablespoons of flour. Allow dough to rest 30 minutes in a covered bowl in a warm place.

Preheat oven to 400 degrees. Cut a piece of parchment paper to fit a 9 x 13-inch jelly roll pan. Lay paper on work surface and lightly flour. Roll dough out on floured paper until dough measures 8 x 12 inches. Filling ingredients will be layered vertically down the center, leaving a 3-inch border on both sides. Spread pesto down this center, followed by a layer of sun-dried tomatoes, mozzarella and Parmesan cheeses, and olives. With a knife, make slits on both sides at 45 degree angles all the way down. Fold each flap towards center, criss-crossing over the filling. Lift the parchment and stuffed dough onto the jelly roll pan. For the egg wash, lightly beat egg with water and brush over top of bread. Bake for 25 minutes or until golden brown.

TO PLATE: *Place braided bread onto a platter so that braiding is displayed.*

NOTE: *In order to save time, use purchased pizza dough. The braiding makes this bread a showpiece. As for taste, this recipe always proves to be a favorite.*

On an EMUNAH mission, participants were given the opportunity to meet some of the great chefs of Israel. Chef Yocheved Hirsch studied in La Varenne Cooking School in Paris, at the Culinary Institute of America in Hyde Park and at the Institute of Culinary Education in New York City. Yocheved has been teaching cooking classes for more than 20 years in the United States and in Israel.

Wheat Berry and Barley with Mozzarella Cheese

SERVES: 4-6 | PREP TIME: 10 MINUTES PLUS OVERNIGHT SOAKING | COOK TIME: 45 MINUTES

½ cup wheat berries
1½ cups water, divided, plus water for soaking
½ cup pearl barley
2 cloves garlic, minced into a paste with ½ teaspoon salt
3 scallions, finely chopped
¼ cup loosely packed flat-leaf parsley, finely chopped
1 cup frozen corn kernels
2 tablespoons extra virgin olive oil
2 tablespoons balsamic vinegar
½ pound mozzarella cheese, cut into ¼-inch cubes
kosher salt and freshly ground black pepper
1 cup cherry tomatoes, halved

Soak wheat berries overnight covered with cold water. Drain. Bring ¾ cup water to a boil in a heavy saucepan. Reduce heat and cook until water is absorbed, about 45 minutes. Cool. Meanwhile, place barley into a heavy saucepan with remaining ¾ cup water and bring to a boil. Reduce heat and continue cooking until water is absorbed. Cool. Combine both grains in a large bowl. Add garlic paste, scallions, parsley, corn, oil, vinegar, cheese, salt and pepper to taste. Carefully fold in tomatoes.

TO PLATE: *For individual plating, place a ring mold or a can (with the top and bottom removed) onto a plate. Spoon wheat berry and barley mixture into mold. Lift mold straight up and remove. Alternatively, for family style plating, spoon wheat and barley mixture into a serving bowl.*

NOTE: *Wheat berries are whole, unprocessed wheat kernels. They are high in protein and fiber, but must be soaked and then cooked in order to eat. The crunchy texture of the wheat berry, the chewiness of the barley and corn, the smooth feeling of the mozzarella cheese and the burst of juice in the tomato, create the perfect palate-pleasing combination of this dish.*

The combination of Helen Nash's training by several of the world's renowned cooking personalities and her own innate flair for food, has enabled Helen to be totally successful in creating fabulous gourmet dishes, while strictly adhering to kosher dietary laws. She is the author of three cookbooks and is a culinary journalist for the Orthodox Union's *Jewish Action* magazine.

Scalloped Potatoes

SERVES: 8-9 | PREP TIME: 10 MINUTES | COOK TIME: 1 HOUR 20 MINUTES

- **⅓ cup butter**
- **3½ tablespoons all purpose flour**
- **2 teaspoons salt**
- **¾ teaspoon ground black pepper**
- **1 teaspoon Dijon mustard**
- **½ cup thinly sliced scallions (about 4)**
- **2 teaspoons chopped fresh rosemary**
- **2 teaspoons chopped fresh thyme leaves, divided**
- **2 cups milk**
- **3 pounds (about 6 medium) Yukon Gold potatoes, peeled, sliced ⅛-inch thick and covered in water**
- **1 pound (about 2) sweet potatoes, peeled, sliced ⅛-inch thick**
- **1 cup shredded Cheddar cheese**

Potatoes gratinées, or scalloped potatoes, borrows from the French "au gratin" technique, in which thinly sliced potatoes are cooked in some form of cream sauce — typically with Swiss cheese and garlic. Given the freedom to develop a dairy recipe, we were able to experiment with the potatoes and the cheese. The addition of sweet potatoes adds an interesting flavor and color. We love the creamy, yet sharp, taste from the Cheddar, with just a hint of mustard.

Preheat oven to 375 degrees. Melt butter in saucepan over medium heat; whisk in flour. With a wooden spoon, stir in salt, pepper, mustard, scallions, rosemary and 1 teaspoon thyme. Add milk. Continue stirring until sauce thickens and comes to a full boil. Remove from heat. Drain potatoes. Spray a 9-inch square baking pan with non-stick cooking spray. Layer half of Yukon Gold potatoes in bottom of pan. Top with one-third of sauce. Arrange sweet potatoes on top, using all of the sweet potatoes. Top with half of the remaining sauce. Repeat with remaining Yukon Gold potatoes. Add remaining sauce. Top with cheese. Bake, covered, until potatoes are tender, about 1¼ hours. Uncover and broil for an additional 5 minutes. Cut into squares.

TO PLATE: *Serve 1 square per person. Garnish with remaining 1 teaspoon thyme.*

NOTE: *Yukon Gold potatoes contain a moderate amount of starch and moisture and are therefore the preferred ingredient to be used for scalloped potatoes. Regardless of its title — scalloped potatoes, pommes de terre au gratin or gratin dauphinois — this recipe is sure to be a pleaser.*

A wooden spoon is frequently used in a professional kitchen because it is rounded, smooth, relatively soft, does not conduct heat and is non-abrasive. This means that a wooden spoon, when compared to a metal one, is less cumbersome to hold, allows food to be blended rather than cut, will not get hot when used during the cooking process and will not scratch a non-stick pot. A metal spoon is harder and sharper, with an action which can potentially cut ingredients, rather than just blending them. A plastic "wooden spoon" has become popular and can be used in place of a wooden spoon providing that it is heat resistant when using with hot food preparations.

Greek Salad Pizza

SERVES: 6-12 | PREP TIME: 15 MINUTES PLUS 1 HOUR FOR RISING | COOK TIME: 15 MINUTES

PIZZA DOUGH

1 package (2¼ teaspoons) active dry yeast

1 cup warm water

1 teaspoon sugar

3 cups all purpose flour, plus more if necessary

1½ teaspoons salt

1½ tablespoons olive oil plus oil for bowl

TOPPING

½ cup chopped basil

½ teaspoon dried oregano

¼ cup (2-ounces) crumbled feta cheese, divided

¼ cup mayonnaise

2 tablespoons milk

¼ teaspoon ground black pepper

12 ounces (1 small head) romaine lettuce, shredded

¼ cup diced red onion

1 cup diced red bell pepper

¼ cup pitted kalamata olives, halved

In a bowl of food processor, add yeast with water and sugar. After 5 minutes add flour and salt. While machine is on, add oil. Process until dough forms a ball; it should be soft but not sticky. If too sticky, add a bit more flour. Transfer ball to a lightly floured work surface and knead for 2-3 minutes, adding enough additional flour, if necessary, to form a smooth, elastic dough. Transfer to a lightly oiled 2 or 3-quart bowl and turn dough to coat with oil. Cover with a damp towel; let rise in a warm place until doubled in size, about 1 hour.

Preheat oven to 425 degrees. Spray an 11 x 16-inch jelly roll pan with non-stick cooking spray. Roll dough on a floured surface to fit pan. Place dough in pan and sprinkle with basil, oregano and half of feta cheese. Bake until golden brown, about 15 minutes. While dough is baking, whisk mayonnaise, milk, black pepper and remaining feta cheese together to make a dressing. Remove crust from oven. Top with lettuce, onion, red bell pepper and olives. Pour dressing over lettuce. Cut into 12 rectangular pieces.

What does a chef prepare for his/her family on a day off, that is quick, not too much fuss, but still special enough for family and friends? This pizza is one such creation in which the flavors of the dressing and the vegetables are fabulous. The alternative caramelized onion topping is equally delicious.

ALTERNATIVE CARAMELIZED ONION TOPPING

- **2 tablespoons olive oil**
- **3 onions, chopped**
- **1 tablespoon brown sugar**
- **2 tablespoons balsamic vinegar**
- **½ teaspoon salt**
- **½ teaspoon ground black pepper**
- **4 ounces goat cheese, diced**
- **4 ounces mozzarella cheese, grated**
- **1 teaspoon dried oregano**

Preheat oven to 400 degrees. Prepare dough according to directions or use purchased pizza dough. Heat oil in a large deep skillet over medium-high heat. Add onions and cook for about 10 minutes, or until wilted and starting to brown. Add sugar, vinegar, salt and pepper. Reduce heat and cook gently, uncovered, for 15-25 minutes, or until richly caramelized. Cool.

Prick rolled-out dough with a fork in about 12 places. Top with onions and goat and mozzarella cheeses. Sprinkle with oregano. Bake until golden brown, about 15 minutes. Cut into 12 rectangular pieces.

TO PLATE: *Serve 1-2 rectangles on each plate. As an alternative, try making individual pizzas.*

NOTE: *This pizza can be baked on a round pizza pan and then cut into triangles, or baked on a rectangular pan and then sliced into rectangles. Regardless of the shape, it is best straight from the oven. To make in advance, prepare the dough (or purchase commercially prepared dough) and the topping, then assemble and bake just before serving.*

Home-Made Manicotti with Ricotta Cheese and Tomato Sauce

SERVES: 4 | PREP TIME: 10 MINUTES | COOK TIME: 1 HOUR

CRÊPE

1 cup all purpose flour

1½ cups water

3 eggs

1 teaspoon canola oil

½ teaspoon salt

⅓ cup mixed chopped parsley, chives and thyme

oil for pan

SAUCE

2 (14-ounce) cans plum tomatoes with juice, imported from Italy

1 teaspoon salt

¼ cup tomato paste

½ cup chopped basil

6 fresh ripe plum tomatoes, peeled, seeded and diced

FILLING

1 (16-ounce) container ricotta cheese

½ cup grated mozzarella cheese

½ cup grated Parmesan cheese, divided

1 tablespoon chopped parsley

1 teaspoon salt

⅛ teaspoon ground black pepper

GARNISH

4 sprigs flat-leaf parsley

For crêpes, in a food processor, combine flour, water, eggs, oil and salt. Process until smooth, about 20 seconds. Stir in herbs by hand. Set aside.

For sauce, with your hand, squeeze the canned tomatoes in a pot. Add salt, tomato paste and basil. Simmer, stirring for 20 minutes. Add fresh tomatoes and simmer an additional 5 minutes.

In a bowl, combine ricotta, mozzarella and ¼ cup Parmesan cheese, parsley, salt and pepper.

Heat an 8-inch, non-stick sauté pan over medium heat. Brush pan with oil. Add ¼ cup crêpe batter and swirl pan until batter covers bottom of pan. When set, after about 3 minutes, loosen edges and turn upside down on a plate. Repeat, totaling 8 crêpes.

Preheat oven to 350 degrees. To assemble, spread 2 cups of sauce on bottom of baking dish. Spoon 2 tablespoons of filling on one edge of each crêpe; roll like a jelly roll. Arrange seam-side down in baking dish in a single layer. Top with remaining sauce. Bake 20 minutes.

TO PLATE: *Place 2 manicotti rolls on a plate. Spoon sauce on top. Sprinkle with remaining Parmesan cheese. Garnish with parsley sprig.*

NOTE: *Since this recipe is time consuming, consider preparing and refrigerating the sauce and crêpes a day in advance. If storing, be sure to wrap crêpes well in plastic wrap, as they will dry out.*

When purchasing canned tomatoes, chefs choose San Marzano, grown in a region of Southern Italy, with a rich volcanic soil mix. The soil, kissed by the Mediterranean sun, ensures a sugar-infused tomato that only nature can create.

Marie Rizzuto, an established home-style Italian chef, was family trained. Her legacy of recipes dates back to her ancestors in Bari, Italy. Friends and family alike look forward to any catered meal by this great chef.

pasta

Fettuccini with Tomatoes,
Olives and Parmesan Cheese

Orzo with Garbanzo Beans, Red Onion,
Basil and Mint

Spaghetti with
Fresh Tomato Sauce and Basil

Cavatappi with Butternut Squash
and Dried Cranberries

Colorful Couscous

Fusilli Pasta with Gazpacho Sauce

Angel Hair Pasta with Soffritto Infused Cod

Acini De Pepe with
Butter and Chickpeas — Cascasoon

Farfalle Pasta with
Asparagus and Sun-Dried Tomatoes

Tortellini à la Vodka

Fettuccini with Tomatoes, Olives and Parmesan Cheese

SERVES: 8 | PREP TIME: 10 MINUTES | COOK TIME: 12 MINUTES

1 (16-ounce) package fettuccini
6 tablespoons olive oil
½ cup drained sun-dried tomatoes packed in oil
¼ cup red wine vinegar
1 tablespoon drained capers
1 clove garlic, minced
½ pint yellow cherry tomatoes, halved
½ pint red cherry tomatoes, halved
½ cup minced, pitted, oil-cured black olives
2 tablespoons fresh chives, minced
1 cup fresh basil leaves, thinly sliced
1 cup freshly grated Parmesan cheese
salt and freshly ground black pepper

Cook pasta al dente, according to directions on box. Meanwhile, put oil, sun-dried tomatoes, vinegar, capers and garlic in a food processor and coarsely chop. Drain pasta; transfer to a large bowl. Add sun-dried tomato mixture to hot pasta; toss to coat. Add yellow and red tomatoes, olives, chives, basil and Parmesan cheese. Season to taste with salt and pepper.

TO PLATE: *With a large serving fork twist pasta into a spiral. Place on individual plate; remove fork by lifting it straight up. Alternatively, serve family style on a platter or in a shallow pasta bowl.*

NOTE: *Never add oil to the cooking water, just salt. Stir the pasta to prevent sticking. In a restaurant, pasta is cooked about 90 percent of the way through in boiling, salted water. It is then finished in a sauté pan with a little bit of the pasta water and the sauce. The starchiness of the cooking water helps the sauce adhere to the pasta.*

The vibrant colors of this dish become especially highlighted when served on a white serving platter.

When the administration in Washington, D.C. invited esteemed guests to share in the celebration of Israel's 50th Independence Day, it came as no surprise that Moshe Bassoon, an internationally recognized chef, was selected to prepare dinner. As the renowned restaurateur and chef of Eucalyptus in Israel, Chef Bassoon focuses on using ingredients that can be collected from the surrounding Jerusalem hills. Chef Bassoon has won many international awards including one from *Food & Wine Magazine* which elected Eucalyptus as one of the six best restaurants around the globe. This chef is also known for his philanthropic work, creating soup kitchens, where "dignity is dished out with every meal."

Orzo with Garbanzo Beans, Red Onion, Basil and Mint

SERVES: 6 | PREP TIME: 10 MINUTES | COOK TIME: 7 MINUTES

RED WINE VINAIGRETTE

½ cup red wine vinegar
¼ cup fresh lemon juice
2 teaspoons honey
2 teaspoons salt
¾ teaspoon ground black pepper
1 cup extra virgin olive oil

ORZO

4 cups parve chicken broth or water
½ cup orzo
1 (15-ounce) can garbanzo beans, rinsed and drained
1½ cups mixed red and yellow teardrop tomatoes or grape tomatoes, halved
¾ cup finely chopped red onion
½ cup chopped fresh basil
¼ cup chopped fresh mint
salt and freshly ground black pepper

Mix vinegar, lemon juice, honey, salt and pepper in a blender. With machine running, gradually blend in oil. Season vinaigrette to taste with more salt and pepper, if desired. Set aside.

Bring broth to a boil in a large, heavy saucepan over high heat. Stir in orzo. Cover partially and cook, stirring frequently, until orzo is tender but still firm to the bite, about 7 minutes. Drain orzo through a strainer. Transfer to a large, wide bowl and toss until orzo cools slightly. Set aside to cool completely. Toss orzo with beans, tomatoes, onion, basil, mint and enough vinaigrette to coat; you may not need entire amount prepared. Season to taste with salt and pepper.

TO PLATE: *Spoon orzo into a bowl and serve at room temperature.*

NOTE: *Ripe tomatoes, fresh basil and fragrant mint all come together in this dish in celebration of the arrival of long, warm summer days.*

Giada De Laurentiis has become known as America's favorite celebrity Italian cook and cookbook author. Born in Rome, Italy, she began her culinary career at Le Cordon Bleu in Paris. She worked in several restaurants including Wolfgang Puck's Spago. Later, she started her own catering company. This recipe was given to us from the chef's book, *Giada's Family Dinners* (Clarkson Potter — Random House).

Spaghetti with Fresh Tomato Sauce and Basil

SERVES: 4 | PREP TIME: 20 MINUTES | COOK TIME: 25 MINUTES

20 ripe plum tomatoes
⅓ cup extra virgin olive oil
pinch of crushed red pepper
kosher salt
freshly ground black pepper
1 (16-ounce) package spaghetti
1 tablespoon unsalted butter
12-16 fresh basil leaves stacked and rolled into a cylinder, cut thinly crosswise
½ cup freshly grated Parmesan cheese

To peel tomatoes, bring a large pot of water to a boil. Have a large bowl of ice water nearby. Cut a small X on the bottom of each tomato. Add tomatoes to pot, boil 15 seconds. Promptly remove tomatoes and place them in ice water for 1 minute. Pull off skin with the tip of a paring knife. Cut tomatoes in half and remove seeds. To cook tomatoes, in a wide pan, heat oil over medium-high heat until hot. Add tomatoes, crushed red pepper and season lightly with salt and pepper. Remember that as the liquid in the tomato sauce reduces, salt will become concentrated. Let tomatoes cook for a few minutes to soften. Then, using a potato masher, chop tomatoes finely. Cook sauce until thickened, about 20-25 minutes. To serve, cook spaghetti according to instructions on package, 1 minute less than al dente. Reserve a little pasta cooking water. Add pasta to sauce and cook over medium-high heat. Using two wooden spoons, gently toss pasta and sauce together. If sauce seems too thick, add a little pasta cooking water to it. Take pan off heat; toss butter, basil and cheese with pasta in same manner. The pasta should take on an orange hue.

TO PLATE: *Serve in warmed pasta bowls with extra grated cheese.*

NOTE: *This homemade tomato sauce prepared with fresh tomatoes is a special treat. The best time to make this dish is during the late summer, when tomatoes are at their peak. The easiest way to seed plum tomatoes is to cut them around the equator from the shorter side, not lengthwise. The seeds can easily be flicked out with your finger tip or a spoon.*

The water in which the pasta is cooked is an important ingredient in any pasta recipe and a portion of it should always be reserved. If the pasta is dry after it has been tossed with sauce, pasta water can be added. The benefit is twofold: not only does this aid in moistening the pasta, but also, the starch left behind acts as a binder between the sauce and pasta.

A James Beard Award recipient, Scott Conant, of L'Impero and Alto in Manhattan, has *Gourmet* magazine raving that "Conant raises the roof on the Manhattan school of Italian cooking." Chef Conant showcases this pasta from *Scott Conant's New Italian Cooking* (Conant and McAllister Smart: Broadway).

Cavatappi with Butternut Squash and Dried Cranberries

SERVES: 4 | PREP TIME: 20 MINUTES | COOK TIME: 30 MINUTES

- **½ (16-ounce package) cavatappi pasta**
- **2 tablespoons extra virgin olive oil, plus extra for sprinkling**
- **1 medium onion, ¼-inch dice**
- **2 pounds butternut squash, peeled, seeded, ¾-inch dice**
- **½ teaspoon ground cinnamon**
- **⅛ teaspoon ground nutmeg**
- **salt and freshly ground black pepper**
- **¾ cup vegetable broth**
- **¼ cup dried cranberries**
- **2 tablespoons honey**
- **2 teaspoons lemon juice**
- **1 tablespoon chopped fresh mint, divided, plus sprigs for garnish**
- **¼ cup roasted pumpkin seeds**

Cook pasta al dente, according to directions on package. Reserve ½ cup cooking liquid before draining pasta. Meanwhile, heat oil in a large saucepan. Add onion; sauté over medium heat for 4 minutes. Add squash, cinnamon, nutmeg, salt and pepper. Cover and cook over low heat, stirring occasionally for 5 minutes. Add broth. Simmer, covered, until squash is barely tender, about 12-15 minutes. If necessary, add a few tablespoons of water to prevent burning. Add cranberries, honey, lemon juice and 2 teaspoons mint. Cook for additional 5 minutes. Add pasta to squash, tossing over low heat for 1 minute. If needed, add pasta liquid, a few tablespoons at a time, to moisten. Season to taste with salt and pepper.

TO PLATE: *Spoon pasta onto plate. Sprinkle with oil, pumpkin seeds and remaining 1 teaspoon mint. Garnish with mint sprig.*

Faye Levy, culinary columnist and author of fourteen cookbooks in three languages, received her formal training at La Varenne Cooking School in Paris. She is a James Beard Award recipient and a three-time winner of the prestigious Tastemaker Award from the International Association of Culinary Professionals. Her creative dishes have appeared on the covers of America's top cooking magazines. A variation of this recipe, created by this superb chef, appeared in the *International Jerusalem Post.*

Colorful Couscous

SERVES: 8-10 | PREP TIME: 15 MINUTES | COOK TIME: 5 MINUTES

- **1 cup couscous or Israeli couscous**
- **½ cup black raisins**
- **1 (15-ounce) can chickpeas, drained and rinsed**
- **3 scallions, chopped**
- **1 red bell pepper, ¼-inch dice**
- **1 zucchini, ¼-inch dice**
- **½ cup ¼-inch diced mango or papaya**
- **¼ cup lemon juice**
- **¼ cup extra virgin olive oil**
- **1 clove garlic, chopped**
- **1 teaspoon cumin**
- **½ teaspoon turmeric**
- **¼ teaspoon hot red pepper sauce**
- **¼ cup chopped parsley**
- **salt and freshly ground black pepper**

Prepare couscous according to package directions. Add raisins, chickpeas, scallions, red bell pepper, zucchini and mango or papaya. In a separate small bowl, whisk lemon juice, oil, garlic, cumin, turmeric and hot pepper sauce. Pour mixture over couscous. Add parsley and toss to combine; adjust salt and pepper to taste.

TO PLATE: *Serve room temperature in a bowl that will allow the colors of this couscous salad to be the focal point.*

NOTE: *Traditional couscous is a coarsely ground semolina pasta that is a staple in many North African countries. It is labor-intensive to prepare from scratch. In the market, quick-cooking couscous is readily available and easy to use. An alternative ingredient for this recipe is Israeli couscous, which was used in the photograph. Israeli couscous is a uniform size, short-cut pasta. Regardless of the couscous selected, for aesthetics, all ingredients that are diced should be approximately the same size as the chickpeas.*

After testing many couscous recipes, we combined what we liked most from each, ultimately creating a recipe that we confidently recommend as the best of the best. The colors and taste cannot be beat.

Fusilli Pasta with Gazpacho Sauce

SERVES: 6 | PREP TIME: 15 MINUTES | COOK TIME: 10 MINUTES

PASTA AND SAUCE

- **1 (16-ounce) box fusilli pasta**
- **5 plum tomatoes, seeded**
- **1 seedless cucumber, peeled**
- **1 red bell pepper, seeded, reserving ½ for garnish**
- **1 jalapeño pepper, seeded, reserving ½ for garnish**
- **2 cloves garlic, smashed**
- **½ cup chopped red onion**
- **¼ teaspoon ground cumin**
- **pinch cayenne pepper**
- **1¾ teaspoons kosher salt**
- **½ teaspoon ground black pepper**
- **½ teaspoon lime juice**
- **¼ cup dried breadcrumbs**
- **½ cup extra virgin olive oil**

GARNISH

- **1 avocado, ¼-inch dice**
- **cilantro sprigs**

Cook pasta al dente, according to directions on box. In a food processor, purée tomatoes, cucumber, ½ red bell pepper, ½ jalapeño pepper, garlic, onion, cumin, cayenne pepper, salt, black pepper, lime juice and breadcrumbs. With machine running, add oil in thin stream. Toss drained pasta with sauce. For garnish, cut remaining half red bell pepper and half jalapeño pepper into ⅛-inch dice.

TO PLATE: *Spoon pasta onto plate. Garnish with avocado, red bell and jalapeño peppers, and sprig of cilantro. Serve at room temperature.*

NOTE: *Gazpacho, one of the most famous dishes of Spanish cuisine, exemplifies sunshine, vibrant color and easy living. There is no need to worry about knife skills here, since the sauce is prepared simply by pushing the button of a food processor. This is a delightful summer pasta.*

In many restaurants, the line chefs' responsibilities include preparing staff meals. It is not long before a competition ensues to determine who can prepare the easiest and most well-received dish. Gazpacho on a hot summer day is always popular. This recipe was created when the outside temperature soared and the kitchen felt like a sauna. It turned out to be extremely popular and refreshing, and a frequently requested dish.

Angel Hair Pasta with Soffritto Infused Cod

SERVES: 4 | PREP TIME: 5-10 MINUTES | COOK TIME: 25 MINUTES

2 tablespoons olive oil
⅓ cup finely chopped yellow onion
2 cloves garlic, chopped
½ cup white wine
1 (14.5-ounce) can diced tomatoes, undrained
½ pound boneless, skinless cod, cut into ½-inch cubes
salt and freshly ground black pepper
½ pound angel hair pasta
3 tablespoons chopped flat-leaf parsley

Preheat oven to 375 degrees. In an oven-safe sauté pan, heat oil, onion and garlic over medium heat. Sauté 5 minutes. Add wine, increase heat to high. Stir in tomatoes. When sauce comes to a boil, remove from heat. Season fish with salt and pepper. Add fish to pan with sauce, spooning sauce over fish. Put pan into oven and bake until fish is firm and opaque, about 15 minutes. Adjust seasoning with salt and pepper to taste. Cook pasta in boiling, salted water for 5 minutes. Drain. Gently combine cod, sauce and pasta.

TO PLATE: *Firmly grasp a serving of pasta with tongs. Place the tongs perpendicular to the pan and, using the tip, twirl the pasta into a turban shape. Slide the twisted pasta from the pan onto the serving plate. Sprinkle with chopped parsley.*

NOTE: *Soffritto is a mixture of finely-chopped aromatics, such as onion and garlic, that are sautéed in olive oil. Soffritto serves as a base for many dishes. The chef recommends putting garlic into room temperature oil in the sauté pan, and then heating both together to avoid the bitter taste that garlic can acquire when it is overcooked. Feel free to substitute haddock or sea bass for the cod.*

With everything he does, Moshe David reaffirms his commitment and dedication to the highest standards of glatt kosher catering to the Jewish community. Moshe's catering boutique, Fig and Palm, a joint venture with Arthur Backal (a recognized and established figure in the New York hotel and catering industry), highlights their mantra: each event, large or small, is approached in a unique and creative manner with their professional and personal touch.

Acini De Pepe with Butter and Chickpeas — Cascasoon

SERVES: 6-8 | PREP TIME: 5 MINUTES | COOK TIME: 40 MINUTES

- **1 onion, chopped (about ½ cup)**
- **¼ cup vegetable oil**
- **1 (16-ounce) package acini de pepe pasta, orzo, or Israeli couscous**
- **1 (15-ounce) can chickpeas, rinsed and drained**
- **2½ teaspoons kosher salt**
- **3½ cups water**
- **4 tablespoons unsalted butter**
- **2 tablespoons chopped parsley**
- **½ pound Cheddar or Muenster cheese, shredded**

Preheat oven to 350 degrees. In a medium, heavy-bottom saucepan, sauté onion in oil over medium heat until translucent, about 4 minutes. Add pasta and continue sautéing for 4 minutes, stirring intermittently. Add chickpeas, salt and water. Bring to a boil. Reduce heat to low and simmer, covered, until water is absorbed, about 15-20 minutes. Add butter and chopped parsley; toss gently. Pour cascasoon into a 2½-quart casserole dish. Top with cheese. Bake until cheese melts, about 10 minutes.

TO PLATE: *Serve in large bowl or in individual gratin serving dishes.*

NOTE: *If you do not use a heavy-bottom saucepan, the pasta will stick to the bottom of the pot.*

The name of this dish, cascasoon, translates to mean "minced into small pieces" (perfectly describing the tiny pasta). It shares the same etymology as North Africa's couscous. Cascasoon is a long-time favorite for evening dairy meals.

Poopa Dweck, an expert on Aleppian Jewish cookery, is the creator of Deal Delights and most recently, the author of the magnificent coffee table cookbook, *Aromas of Aleppo — The Legendary Cuisine of Syrian Jews. Aromas of Aleppo* is an extraordinary collection of the culinary treasures and soulful customs of the ancient, yet enduring, Aleppian Jewish community. In the words of Poopa Dweck, "sifrah daimeh — may your table always be plentiful!"

Farfalle Pasta with Asparagus and Sun-Dried Tomatoes

SERVES: 6 | PREP TIME: 5 MINUTES | COOK TIME: 15 MINUTES

- **1 (16-ounce) box farfalle pasta**
- **1 large onion, cut in half, thinly sliced into half rounds**
- **2 teaspoons olive oil**
- **1 teaspoon chopped garlic**
- **1 bunch asparagus, cut into 2-inch pieces on diagonal**
- **1 (10-ounce) jar roasted red peppers, drained, rinsed and ⅛-inch dice**
- **1 (8-ounce) jar sun-dried tomatoes packed in oil, cut into quarters**
- **2 teaspoons salt plus more to taste**
- **2 teaspoons sugar**

Cook pasta al dente, according to directions on box. In the meantime, in a large sauté pan over medium-high heat, sauté onion in oil for 4 minutes. Add garlic and continue to sauté for 1 minute. Remove from pan and set aside. Add asparagus to same pan; sauté 3 minutes. Add red pepper, tomatoes, salt, sugar and reserved sautéed onions with garlic. Remove from heat. Combine with pasta. Adjust seasoning with salt to taste.

TO PLATE: *Serve warm or at room temperature in a decorative bowl.*

NOTE: *"Al dente" from the Italian "to the teeth" describes pasta that is cooked until it is soft enough to eat, but not overdone.*

Since pastas come in an astonishing variety of shapes, when using a chunkier sauce, sturdier pasta is selected. Bowties, also known as butterflies, from the Italian "farfalla," have been selected for this recipe because of their sturdy shape.

Looking for new ideas, a chef relies on professional publications and high-end magazines for inspiration. A variation of this recipe, appearing in *Food and Wine Magazine*, served as the springboard for this easy, colorful and flavorful dish.

Tortellini à la Vodka

SERVES: 4 | PREP TIME: 10 MINUTES | COOK TIME: 1 HOUR 20 MINUTES

- **1 medium onion, ¼-inch dice**
- **1 clove garlic, minced**
- **¼ cup olive oil**
- **1 carrot, ⅛-inch dice**
- **1 (28-ounce) can crushed tomatoes**
- **1 bay leaf**
- **1½ cups heavy cream**
- **½ cup grated Parmesan cheese**
- **2 tablespoons vodka**
- **salt and freshly ground black pepper**
- **1 (16-ounce) package frozen cheese tortellini**
- **¼ cup chopped flat-leaf parsley, plus sprigs for garnish**

In a large, deep saucepan, sauté onion and garlic in oil, stirring periodically until softened, about 5 minutes. Add carrot and sauté an additional 5 minutes. Add tomatoes and bay leaf. Simmer, uncovered, over low heat for 1 hour, stirring every so often. Shortly before sauce is finished cooking, place cream into a large sauté pan over medium-low heat. Allow cream to simmer. Add Parmesan cheese and simmer an additional 5 minutes. Remove bay leaf from red sauce. Add cream mixture to red sauce along with vodka. Stir well. Simmer 5 minutes. Season with salt and pepper to taste. Cook tortellini according to package directions; drain. Add sauce and combine well.

TO PLATE: *Spoon tortellini with sauce into a shallow gratin dish. Sprinkle with chopped parsley. Garnish with parsley sprig.*

NOTE: *If you are interested in a traditional penne à la vodka dish, feel free to substitute penne for the tortellini.*

Chefs prefer flat-leaf Italian parsley to curly because it is sweeter and less bitter.

Whether catering to hundreds of people or a family of six, everyone is looking for shortcuts to speed up the cooking process. A professional chef would prepare a much more sophisticated version of this dish. However, there are times when quick, easy and delicious are the priority. In its original form, tortellini, which means little twists, would be prepared by pinching two corners together from home-made ravioli. Chopped heirloom tomatoes, from the farmer's market, would be featured instead of the canned crushed tomatoes. We have prepared this variation using ready-made tortellini and have decided that it too, is praiseworthy. Without a doubt, there will be requests for seconds.

sides

Potato Purée with Herbed Potato Chip

Chinese Style Broccoli

Brown Rice with Cremini Mushrooms,
Carrots, Dried Cranberries and Pecans

Mediterranean Style Stuffed Bell Pepper

Roasted Garlic Pommes Anna

Sautéed Spinach with Pine Nuts and Raisins

Tuscan New Potatoes

Marinated Eggplant

Honeyed Butternut Squash

Edamame, String Bean,
Snow Pea and Tomato Salad

Potato Purée with Herbed Potato Chip

SERVES: 6 | PREP TIME: 20 MINUTES | COOK TIME: 40 MINUTES

HERBED POTATO CHIP

- vegetable oil
- 1 (8-ounce) russet potato, do not soak in water
- 6 sprigs of thyme, sage, parsley or herb of your choice
- kosher salt

Preheat oven to 350 degrees. Brush a silpat or parchment paper with oil placed on a cookie sheet or jelly roll pan. Using a mandoline, slice russet potato paper thin, arranging 8 slices in a single layer. Center a small herb sprig or some of the leaves onto each potato slice, ensuring that there remains a ½-inch border around the edges of the slice. Cover with slice that is similar in size. Press sides together to seal in herbs and remove air pockets. Brush with oil. Bake 6 minutes. Flip over; bake an additional 3 minutes. Allow to cool. Sprinkle with salt.

POMMES PURÉES

- 2 pounds Yukon Gold potatoes
- coarse sea salt
- 1¼ cups whole milk or non-dairy soy milk, heated
- 16 tablespoons of butter or margarine, chilled, and cut into small pieces, divided

For pommes purées, scrub potatoes but do not peel. Place potatoes in a large saucepan and fill with enough cold water to cover by at least 1 inch. For each quart of water, add 1 tablespoon of salt. Simmer, uncovered, over medium heat until a knife inserted into potato comes away without resistance, about 20-30 minutes. Drain potatoes as soon as they are cooked. Meanwhile, in a large saucepan, bring milk to just a boil over high heat. Set aside. Once potatoes are cool enough to handle, peel them and cut into manageable pieces. Pass potatoes through finest grid of a ricer or food mill into a large, heavy-bottomed saucepan. Place pan over low heat, and with a wooden spatula, stir potatoes vigorously to dry them, 4-5 minutes. Begin adding 12 tablespoons butter, little by little, stirring quickly until each batch of butter is thoroughly incorporated and mixture becomes fluffy and light. Slowly add about three-fourths of hot milk in a thin stream, stirring continuously, until milk is thoroughly absorbed. Place over low heat and stir well. If purée seems a bit heavy and stiff, add some of remaining butter and milk, whisking constantly. Taste for seasoning and adjust with salt.

TO PLATE: *Serve individual portion with herbed potato chip standing up as a garnish.*

NOTE: *Boiling potatoes with their skin on prevents them from absorbing too much water. The best mashing tool is a ricer, with a food mill a close second; a potato masher or fork is fine too. Avoid a food processor because it makes the potatoes gummy. To keep potato purée warm for at least half an hour, place in a heat-proof bowl, covered with plastic wrap, and set over a pot of simmering water.*

The garnish is something learned while in culinary school and will surely have your guests wondering how it is made. For the herbed chip, it is the starch in the potato that helps seal the "sandwich," so do not rinse the potato slices or put them in water to soak. This garnish, which is intended more for aesthetics, can be made up to two days in advance and stored in an airtight container.

The legacy of Joel Robuchon is that of a chef who took the great canon of French cooking, thoroughly steeped himself in its wisdom, then redefined it through a bold exploration of new flavors, influences, ingredients and techniques. In 1981, Robuchon opened Jamin, his first restaurant, as executive chef/owner. Jamin was awarded three Michelin stars within two years of opening. Other restaurants include: Joel Robuchon, Robuchon A Galera in Macau, L'Atelier de Joel Robuchon and L'Atelier de Joel Robuchon at the Four Seasons Hotel in Manhattan. His pommes purées, or mashed potatoes, a humble sounding dish that acquired near-cult-status, exemplifies one of his basic cooking principles: "To make a grand meal, you have to make it simple. To look simple is very complicated. You have to have the highest quality products, the best equipment and you have to keep the focus on the original flavor of the product."

Chinese Style Broccoli

SERVES: 4 | PREP TIME: 10 MINUTES | COOK TIME: 10 MINUTES

2 teaspoons sesame seeds
2½ pounds broccoli florets
½ cup orange juice
¼ cup brown sugar
¼ cup soy sauce
1 tablespoon cornstarch
3 tablespoons minced garlic
2 teaspoons minced ginger
2 tablespoons sesame oil
1 teaspoon grated orange zest
¼ teaspoon red pepper flakes

Heat a dry frying pan over medium-low heat. When warm, add sesame seeds in a single layer. Periodically remove pan from flame and shake pan to keep seeds from jumping out of pan and to prevent burning. When seeds begin to release a scent, after 1-2 minutes, they are ready. Remove from pan to cool. Add broccoli to a pot of salted, boiling water. Cook 3 minutes. Drain and immerse immediately into a large bowl of ice water. Drain well. Set aside. In another bowl, combine orange juice, brown sugar, soy sauce and cornstarch; set aside. In a sauté pan over medium heat, sauté garlic and ginger in sesame oil for 30 seconds. Add orange juice combination; cook until thick, about 1 minute. Pour sauce over broccoli and toss.

TO PLATE: *Transfer broccoli to a platter and garnish with orange zest, red pepper flakes and toasted sesame seeds.*

NOTE: *Blanching cooks the broccoli just enough to heighten its flavor and intensify the color. Blanching is simply cooking food very briefly in boiling water and then submerging it in ice water to stop the cooking process.*

Sesame seeds, because of their high oil content, can quickly become rancid. It is best to store them in an airtight container in the refrigerator or freezer.

When purchasing garlic, avoid heads with small green sprouts. Store in a cool, dry place. To avoid a bitter and unpleasant aftertaste, garlic should never be cooked to a dark-brown color.

Mr. Wong, his son Sam, and daughter-in-law Amy, are the original owners of Wing Wan which means “good fortune.” Initially, the Long Island, New York, restaurant was not kosher. After Mr. Wong spoke to the Rabbi of the community 17 years ago, Wing Wan underwent a metamorphosis and became a thriving kosher business. The owners have become well-versed in the laws of kashrut and Sabbath observance. Through much hard work and “good fortune” they continue to be very successful.

Brown Rice with Cremini Mushrooms, Carrots, Dried Cranberries and Pecans

SERVES: 6-8 | PREP TIME: 12 MINUTES | COOK TIME: 50 MINUTES

½ cup pecan halves
1 cup brown rice
2 tablespoons walnut oil or olive oil
¼ cup red onion, ¼-inch dice
1 celery stalk, ¼-inch dice
1 carrot, ¼-inch dice
¾ cup sliced cremini mushrooms
1 cup dried cranberries
1 teaspoon minced garlic
¾ teaspoon salt
¼ teaspoon ground black pepper
1 tablespoon chopped flat-leaf parsley

Preheat oven to 350 degrees. Place pecans on a jelly roll pan and toast, tossing occasionally, for 7 minutes. Remove from pan to cool. Cook rice according to directions on package. Meanwhile, heat oil in a sauté pan over medium heat. Add onion, celery and carrot; sauté 7 minutes. Add mushrooms, cranberries and garlic; cook an additional 2 minutes. In a large bowl, combine toasted pecans, rice, mushroom mixture, salt and pepper.

TO PLATE: *Spoon into a serving dish and garnish with chopped parsley. Serve warm or at room temperature.*

NOTE: *Cremini mushrooms, more flavorful than white mushrooms, are immature Portobello mushrooms.*

Several years ago, a chef at Rising Tide Natural Market in Glen Cove, New York, shared a version of this recipe. The combination of colors, texture and nutritional benefit is sure to enhance any table.

Mediterranean Style Stuffed Bell Pepper

SERVES: 8 | PREP TIME: 10 MINUTES | COOK TIME: 20 MINUTES

2 small yellow bell peppers, halved lengthwise, seeded
2 small red bell peppers, halved lengthwise, seeded
4 cloves garlic, chopped
¼ cup capers, soaked in water, drained and chopped
½ cup breadcrumbs
¼ cup chopped flat-leaf parsley
¼ cup raisins, soaked in warm water 1 hour
¼ cup pine nuts
1 cup extra virgin olive oil
salt and freshly ground black pepper

Preheat oven to 400 degrees. Place red and yellow bell peppers in an oven-safe dish, cut side up. Bake 5 minutes. Meanwhile, mix garlic, capers, breadcrumbs, parsley, raisins, pine nuts, oil, salt and pepper. Spoon into pepper halves. Return to oven. Bake 15 minutes.

TO PLATE: *Serve alternating red and yellow bell pepper halves on a white platter.*

NOTE: *Whenever you chop garlic, it is useful to sprinkle the garlic and the cutting board with kosher salt which adds friction and resistance, making the garlic easier to chop. When chopping parsley, reserve stems, which can be frozen and used later to flavor soups.*

Chefs Gabriella Mari and Cristina Blasi established the Italian Cordon Bleu Cooking School located in the heart of Florence, a few minutes walk from the Duomo. Participants are encouraged to utilize the well-equipped kitchen laboratory, an extensive gastronomic library, and a wine and food tasting area as Gabriella and Cristina welcome you to their Scuola di Arte Culinaria.

Roasted Garlic Pommes Anna

SERVES: 4 | PREP TIME: 15 MINUTES | COOK TIME: 2 HOURS

- **1 head garlic**
- **4 tablespoons extra virgin olive oil, divided**
- **2¼ teaspoons salt, divided**
- **¼ cup dry white wine**
- **4 russet potatoes, peeled**
- **⅛ teaspoon ground black pepper**
- **1 teaspoon chopped fresh thyme leaves**
- **1 teaspoon chopped fresh chives, plus extra for garnish**
- **1 teaspoon chopped fresh flat-leaf parsley**

Preheat oven to 350 degrees. Cut off the top one-eighth of garlic head and discard. Place garlic in a small baking dish. Drizzle 1 tablespoon oil onto garlic and sprinkle with ¼ teaspoon salt. Pour wine in dish and cover tightly with foil. Roast garlic until cloves are very soft and can be squeezed out of head, about 1 hour. Cool garlic before handling. Squeeze cloves from head and mash with a fork; set aside. Using a mandoline or Asian slicer, slice potatoes into paper-thin rounds. Put cut potatoes into a large bowl and toss with 1 tablespoon oil, mashed garlic, remaining 2 teaspoons salt, pepper, thyme, chives and parsley. Place an oven-safe, 8 or 10-inch sauté pan over medium-low heat. Coat bottom of pan with remaining 2 tablespoons oil. Layer potatoes in pan, overlapping each other in a circle to cover the bottom of the pan. This bottom layer should be evenly spaced, since it will be the presentation side. Add remaining potatoes. Slowly brown potatoes on stove top until bottom layer is golden brown and can be shaken loose, approximately 30 minutes. Invert pan onto a plate, then slide the galette from the plate back into the pan in order to cook the other side. Transfer pan to oven; continue cooking until under side is browned and can be shaken loose, about 30 minutes. Flip galette over onto a cutting board and cut into 4 wedges.

TO PLATE: *Place wedges onto a serving platter. Garnish with chives.*

NOTE: *The French refer to this dish as Pommes Anna; Chef Laura calls it galette. It is easy to prepare, yet yields a professional chef-quality dish. Using a non-stick pan guarantees easy flipping. If this recipe becomes a staple in your home, Chef Laura asserts that a dedicated galette pan should be amongst your kitchen equipment.*

The mandoline is an irreplaceable kitchen utensil that allows slicing of firm vegetables and fruits to be uniform in thickness, which is important for heat distribution in cooking, as well as for presentation. However, it can be dangerous because of its razor-sharp blade and is therefore best used with a metal glove. In addition to slicing, it juliennes, waffle cuts and crinkle cuts.

Laura Frankel is the founder and executive chef of the acclaimed Shallots Bistro in Chicago. After Chef Frankel had a family and began maintaining a kosher home, she discovered that a kosher restaurant, serving the quality food she was confident she could offer, did not exist. To fill this void, Shallots was born. Aside from Shallots Bistro in Chicago, Laura also ran its namesake in New York City for three years. Laura is the author of *Jewish Cooking for All Seasons* (John Wiley & Sons).

Sautéed Spinach with Pine Nuts and Raisins

SERVES: 4-6 | PREP TIME: 10 MINUTES | COOK TIME: 15 MINUTES

- **½ cup black raisins**
- **2 pounds fresh spinach leaves, hard stems removed**
- **2 teaspoons salt**
- **2 tablespoons extra virgin olive oil**
- **1 medium-size yellow onion, finely chopped**
- **½ cup pine nuts**
- **salt and freshly ground black pepper**

In a bowl, soak raisins covered in warm water. Wash spinach well and without draining it, put it in a large sauté pan. Add salt. Cover and cook over medium heat for 5 minutes. Drain and allow to cool. Using your hands, squeeze water from the leaves. Heat oil in a sauté pan over medium heat; add onion. Sauté until soft, about 5 minutes. Add 2 tablespoons of warm water to pan and allow water to evaporate. Add spinach, stir well; decrease heat and simmer for 2 minutes. Add drained raisins and pine nuts. Continue to simmer another 2 minutes. Adjust seasoning with salt and pepper to taste.

TO PLATE: *Serve piled high to form a peak in a bowl, warm or at room temperature.*

NOTE: *This is a traditional dish for the Jewish communities of Rome and Venice. The Sephardic influence is reflected in the combination of pine nuts and raisins in a savory dish, which is not common in Italian cooking. The melding of these flavors was probably brought by the Jews who came from Sicily during the Spanish Inquisition. In addition to its historical significance, this dish is delicious and one that your guests will love!*

Silvia Nacamulli, originally from Italy, is the mastermind behind Cooking For the Soul, in London, England. Going into the food business seemed to be the perfect venue for this chef, as she holds a graduate degree in economics, has experience in the financial world, and developed her culinary craft by carefully observing three generations of fine Italian Jewish cooks. In addition to catering, Silvia also lectures and writes on the history of Italian Jews and Italian Jewish cooking.

Tuscan New Potatoes

SERVES: 4 | PREP TIME: 5 MINUTES PLUS MARINATING TIME | COOK TIME: 40 MINUTES

- **2 pounds new red potatoes**
- **1 tablespoon kosher salt**
- **¼ cup extra virgin olive oil**
- **2 medium-size red onions, peeled and cut into wedges**
- **2 tablespoons capers**
- **3 tablespoons sugar**
- **6 tablespoons white wine vinegar**
- **salt and freshly ground black pepper**
- **1 tablespoon chopped chives for garnish**

Place potatoes and salt in a pot of water. Bring to a boil, lower heat and simmer until potatoes are barely tender when pierced with a paring knife, about 10-15 minutes, depending on size. Drain potatoes in a colander, then place colander with potatoes over the empty pot off the heat. Cover with a clean, dry dish towel. Meanwhile, heat oil in a sauté pan over medium heat. Add onions. Cover pan and continue to sauté over medium-low heat for 15 minutes, stirring every so often. Uncover; add capers and cook 2 minutes. Add sugar; cook additional 3 minutes. Add vinegar; cook 4 minutes more. When potatoes are cool enough to handle, cut them into quarters or halves, depending on size. Place cut potatoes in a large bowl and pour onion mixture over them. Toss well, cover and refrigerate for a few hours to allow flavors to blend. Season to taste with salt and pepper. This dish can be served either warm or at room temperature.

TO PLATE: *Serve on a platter, or in a bowl, garnished with chopped chives.*

NOTE: *Tuscan cuisine refers to food emanating from the Tuscany region of Italy and is synonymous with food that is wonderfully simple, fresh and packed with flavor. A high quality extra virgin olive oil should be used in this recipe, since its taste is a focal point.*

Capers are the flower buds of a bush mostly found in the Mediterranean and are usually pickled in brine and jarred.

New potatoes, low in starch and high in water, with a naturally sweet flavor, are the potatoes of choice when preparing a salad or side dish. Allowing the potatoes to steam after you boil them results in evenly tender, but still firm, potatoes. The combination of sweet, pungent and salty flavors, absorbed by the forever accommodating potato, makes this dish uniquely appealing.

Sandy Mattana, private chef and caterer, resides in Tuscany. Working at the prestigious Cordon Bleu Cooking School in Florence, Italy, as well as for tour groups including A Taste of Tuscany, Chef Sandy continues to please guests with culinary delights, prepared only with the freshest of ingredients.

Marinated Eggplant

SERVES: 4 | PREP TIME: 10 MINUTES PLUS 30 MINUTES FOR DRAINING | COOK TIME: 30 MINUTES

- **1 (1¼-pound) large firm eggplant**
- **2 (4-ounce) ripe plum tomatoes, ¼-inch dice**
- **4 scallions, ½-inch slice**
- **½ small red onion, ¼-inch dice**
- **1 lemon, for zest and juice**
- **1 teaspoon salt**
- **2 tablespoons extra virgin olive oil**
- **½ teaspoon chopped parsley**

Preheat oven to 450 degrees. Prick eggplant with a fork all over skin. Roast in a baking dish until soft, about 20-25 minutes. When cool, discard peel and drain eggplant in a colander for 30 minutes. Put tomatoes, scallions and onion in a bowl. Dice or chop eggplant and add to bowl. In a small bowl, whisk lemon juice, salt and olive oil. Pour over eggplant. Combine well.

TO PLATE: *Spoon into a serving bowl; garnish with chopped parsley and lemon zest.*

NOTE: *Although this recipe, simplistic in form, may appear to be basic, the melding of these fresh Mediterranean flavors, so typical of Israeli cuisine, makes a great dish. In fact, it is one of Chef Shula's daily sell-out items.*

Zest is the outer colored portion of the citrus peel. Use a citrus peeler or a zester to obtain the flavorful shavings. Avoid the white pith as this is bitter. Remember to grate the zest of the fruit first, then squeeze for juice.

Chef Shula came to the United States when she was 18 years old. With a natural flair for the restaurant business, Shula served as both restaurateur and chef. In no time at all, Shula's, on Long Island, quickly enticed its customers with its many signature dishes.

Honeyed Butternut Squash

SERVES: 4-6 | PREP TIME: 10 MINUTES | COOK TIME: 25 MINUTES

2 tablespoons canola oil
2 butternut squash (3-pound total), peeled, seeded and cut in ¾-inch cubes
2 stalks celery, sliced
3 shallots, finely chopped
3 cloves garlic, minced
2 tablespoons honey
¼ teaspoon salt
⅛ teaspoon ground black pepper
¼ cup chopped parsley
¼ cup chopped cilantro

Heat oil in a large sauté pan over medium heat. Add squash, celery, shallots and garlic; sauté 5 minutes. Add honey. Decrease heat; cover and cook 15 minutes. Uncover and continue to cook 5 additional minutes. Add salt and pepper. Toss with parsley and cilantro.

TO PLATE: *Spoon onto a serving platter.*

NOTE: *Shaped like a bowling pin, the bright orange flesh of the squash, with a slightly sweet nuttiness, is challenging to reach because of the protective thick, shiny skin. For stability, use a chef's knife to cut 1 inch from the top and bottom; discard. Using a serrated peeler or the chef's knife, peel away thick skin until you reach the deeper orange flesh of the squash. With a spoon or melon baller, scoop away the seeds and membranes; discard. Cut squash into uniform cubes so that they cook evenly.*

This recipe was acquired on an EMUNAH mission in which we observed the great chefs of Israel produce dishes using the bounties of the land. This particular recipe was served at the Carmel Spa in Haifa.

Edamame, String Bean, Snow Pea and Tomato Salad

SERVES: 4 | PREP TIME: 10 MINUTES | COOK TIME: 7 MINUTES

8 ounces string beans, cut into thirds

6 ounces snow peas, cut in half on diagonal

12 ounces shelled edamame soy beans

12 ounces grape tomatoes, halved

DRESSING

¼ cup red wine vinegar

3 tablespoons extra virgin olive oil

2 teaspoons chopped basil

2 teaspoons chopped thyme

1 teaspoon salt

¾ teaspoon ground black pepper

Place string beans into salted, rapidly boiling water. Cook 3 minutes. Remove string beans, reserving cooking water. Place string beans in ice cold water. Strain and put into a large bowl. Repeat same process for snow peas and edamame, however, only cook snow peas for 30 seconds. Add tomatoes to bowl of vegetables.

In a small bowl, whisk vinegar, oil, basil, thyme, salt and pepper. Dress vegetables just before serving.

TO PLATE: *Spoon into an Oriental-style bowl or dish.*

NOTE: *"Shocking" the vegetables by immersing them in ice water immediately after blanching them in boiling water will ensure that they stay bright green and crisp. Avoid dressing the salad too early otherwise the acid in the vinegar will cause the colors to lose their vibrancy.*

Extra virgin olive oil is often reserved for use with salads, dressings and vinaigrettes because of its distinctive flavor that will not be lost in cooking. The oil should ideally be stored in a stainless steel can or in a tinted dark-colored or porcelain bottle. Air, heat and light will cause the olive oil to turn rancid. A kitchen cabinet, located away from the stove and direct sunlight, provides a good place for storage.

At a luncheon in Los Angeles, California, this beautiful dish was served. It works equally well when plated as a side accompaniment or on a buffet, adding color and texture to any presentation. The burst of flavor speaks for itself.

desserts

Tiramisu

Chocolate Soufflé Roulade
with Coffee Crunch Cream

Poached Pears with
Chocolate Sauce and Toasted Almonds

Decadent Cheesecake

Trilogy: Almond Streusel Topped
Apple Cobbler, Chocolate Mousse-Filled Box
and “Butter” Cookie

Chocolate Bobka

Peanut Butter Mousse Cake

Brownie Cookies

Moist Orange-Pineapple Bundt Cake

Mango Feuillantine

Tiramisu

SERVES: 12 | PREP TIME: 45 MINUTES PLUS OVERNIGHT REFRIGERATION | COOK TIME: 6 MINUTES

2½ cups strong brewed coffee, room temperature
1½ tablespoons coffee liqueur
½ cup dark rum, divided
6 large egg yolks
⅔ cup granulated sugar
¼ teaspoon salt
1 cup heavy cream, chilled, divided
1½ pounds mascarpone cheese
1 teaspoon vanilla extract
1 (14-ounce) package ladyfingers, hard cookie variety
¼ cup cocoa
4 ounces semi- or bittersweet chocolate

Stir brewed coffee, coffee liqueur and ¼ cup rum together in a wide bowl. Set aside. In metal bowl, add yolks, sugar, salt and ¼ cup cream. Set bowl over a medium saucepan containing 1 inch gently simmering water. Cook, constantly scraping along bottom and sides of bowl with a heat-proof spatula, until mixture coats the back of a spoon, about 6 minutes. Remove from heat; stir vigorously to cool slightly. Set aside to allow mixture to reach room temperature, about 15 minutes. Whisk in remaining ¼ cup rum. Add mascarpone; beat with electric mixer until no lumps remain, about 45 seconds. In another bowl, beat remaining ¾ cup cream with vanilla until cream holds stiff peaks. Gently fold whipped cream into mascarpone mixture. Set aside.

To assemble tiramisu, working with one at a time, drop a ladyfinger into coffee mixture so that it floats on the surface, roll over and immediately remove (limited to total of 2-3 seconds). Arrange snugly in single layer in 9 x 13-inch glass baking dish, breaking or trimming ladyfingers as needed to fit neatly into dish. Using a rubber spatula, spread half of mascarpone mixture over ladyfingers, including corners of dish, and then smooth the surface. Place 2 tablespoons cocoa in fine-mesh strainer and dust cocoa over mascarpone. Repeat with a second layer of ladyfingers, remaining mascarpone and cocoa. Cover with plastic wrap and refrigerate a minimum of 6 hours or overnight for the flavors to meld. To serve, cut into rectangles. To shave chocolate, hold chocolate with paper towel, pass vegetable peeler over. Chocolate will curl like wood shavings. To avoid melting, do not touch with fingers.

TO PLATE: *Serve chilled rectangle, sprinkled with cocoa and curled chocolate.*

You too will be shouting "Bravo" when you taste this dessert created by Chef Wael Mazaed of Little Italy in Jerusalem, Israel. Chef Wael was formally trained at the Tadmor School for Hotel Management and continued to learn on the job at Bar Giora. Along with his mentor, Danny Ayash, they create a meeting place that is always included on the itinerary of locals and tourists alike.

Chocolate Soufflé Roulade with Coffee Crunch Cream

SERVES: 8 | PREP TIME: 20 MINUTES PLUS 10 MINUTES FOR COOLING | COOK TIME: 18 MINUTES

CAKE

6 large eggs, separated
¾ cup granulated sugar, divided
¼ cup cocoa, sifted
1 teaspoon vanilla extract
2 tablespoons confectioners' sugar, sifted

Preheat oven to 350 degrees. Spray a 15 x 10-inch jelly roll pan with non-stick cooking spray. Line pan with parchment paper, spray with non-stick cooking spray and dust lightly with flour. In a large bowl, beat egg yolks and ½ cup granulated sugar until light yellow in color. Beat in cocoa and vanilla. In a separate bowl, beat egg whites until foamy. Slowly beat in remaining ¼ cup granulated sugar. Continue beating until whites are stiff. Stir one-fourth of whites into chocolate mixture. Mix well, then fold in remaining whites. Spread chocolate batter evenly over prepared pan. Bake 12-14 minutes, or until puffed and firm to touch. Cool in pan for at least 10 minutes. Dust cake with 2 tablespoons confectioners' sugar, loosen cake from pan and invert onto a clean kitchen towel. Cool completely.

GARNISH

6 ounces bittersweet chocolate

Place a parchment-lined jelly roll pan in the freezer and leave it there until it is very cold, about 1 hour. Melt chocolate in a bowl in microwave on low, checking every 15 seconds. Pour melted chocolate into a small plastic bag. Snip away a tiny corner of the bag. Working on the parchment-lined cold jelly roll pan, make 8 tic-tac-toe, crosshatch or spiral patterns with chocolate. Put into the refrigerator to harden.

COFFEE CRUNCH CREAM FILLING

¾ cup heavy cream or non-dairy whip
2 tablespoons confectioners' sugar
2 tablespoons cocoa
1 teaspoon instant espresso powder or finely ground instant coffee
1½ cups finely chopped Viennese crunch or other toffee chocolate bar

Whip cream in a large bowl. Beat in sugar, cocoa and espresso powder. Spread filling over cake. Sprinkle with Viennese crunch. With your hands, roll the cake up lengthwise or widthwise, then slice.

CHOCOLATE MOCHA SAUCE

- ⅔ cup chopped bittersweet or semi-sweet chocolate
- ½ cup heavy cream or non-dairy whip
- 2 tablespoons strong coffee

Combine chocolate, cream and coffee in a small saucepan and heat gently until melted and smooth. Cool to room temperature.

TO PLATE: *Serve 1 slice on a dessert plate, drizzled with sauce. Lean one chocolate garnish on cake. Feel free to decorate with strawberries, slices of star fruit, confectioners' sugar and sprigs of mint.*

NOTE: *Usually one whisks or mixes with one hand, while the other hand secures the bowl. When additional ingredients need to be added during the mixing process, one way to stabilize the bowl in order to free up your second hand, is to moisten a kitchen towel, roll it into a coil and sit the bowl in this towel nest.*

Toronto's Bonnie Stern is a culinary school director, cookware shop owner, author of multiple cookbooks and a journalist. Not only is she knowledgeable about food, but she also has a knack for being able to share her wealth of information. She is the winner of the International Association of Cooking Professionals Award for the best cookbook — *Bonnie Stern's Essentials of Home Cooking* (Random House, Canada), from which this recipe has been adapted.

Poached Pears with Chocolate Sauce and Toasted Almonds

SERVES: 8 | PREP TIME: 15 MINUTES | COOK TIME: 30 MINUTES

POACHED PEARS

- **4 whole cloves**
- **1 (1-inch) piece ginger, peeled**
- **1 cinnamon stick**
- **½ cup apple cider**
- **½ cup dry white wine**
- **1 cup water**
- **1 cup granulated sugar**
- **1 lemon, sliced**
- **1 orange, sliced**
- **8 medium-size, ripe but firm Forelle or Bartlett pears**

CHOCOLATE SAUCE AND TOASTED ALMONDS

- **6 ounces bittersweet chocolate, roughly chopped**
- **2 tablespoons margarine**
- **⅓ cup boiling water**
- **1 tablespoon corn syrup**
- **2 tablespoons honey**
- **⅓ cup sliced almonds**

For poached pears, place cloves, ginger and cinnamon stick in a piece of cheesecloth and tie. Combine cider, wine, water, sugar, lemon and orange slices and spices in cheesecloth in a pot just big enough to hold pears in an upright position. Bring liquid to a boil, reduce heat and simmer. Meanwhile, peel pears, leaving stems intact. With a melon baller, working from bottom, remove core and seeds. Slice off a small piece from base so pear can stand. Add pears to poaching liquid, stem-side up. Cover and simmer until soft when tested with a sharp knife, about 20-30 minutes. Remove from heat, uncover and cool to room temperature in liquid. If serving later, refrigerate pears in poaching liquid. To complete preparation of dessert, gently remove pears from pot and place on a parchment-lined pan.

Preheat oven to 375 degrees. Prepare sauce by melting chocolate and margarine in a stainless steel bowl over a pot of simmering water. When chocolate has melted, whisk in water, corn syrup and honey. Keep sauce warm. Spread almonds on a jelly roll pan. Toast until lightly brown, about 8-10 minutes. When cool, using your fingers, crumble toasted almonds. Hold pear by stem, gently lower ¾ of pear into chocolate, turning to coat sides. Scatter nuts on top of chocolate covered pear.

TO PLATE: *Place pear on a white plate or platter.*

A beautifully photographed advertisement appearing in a trade magazine was the inspiration behind this recipe. Like Cinderella magically transformed into a radiant princess, here a poached pear undergoes its metamorphosis when served dripping with chocolate and smothered with nuts. The presentation is most dramatic.

Decadent Cheesecake

YIELD: 1 (9-INCH) CAKE | PREP TIME: 35 MINUTES PLUS OVERNIGHT IN REFRIGERATOR | COOK TIME: 1 HOUR

CRUST

1 cup walnuts

1 cup pecans

⅓ cup brown sugar

¼ teaspoon cinnamon

2 tablespoons butter, melted

FILLING

1 cup granulated sugar

3 tablespoons cornstarch

2 pounds cream cheese, room temperature

1½ teaspoons vanilla extract

1 large egg, room temperature

3 egg yolks

½ cup heavy cream

TOPPING

1¼ cups sour cream

3 tablespoons granulated sugar

1 teaspoon vanilla extract

GARNISH

raspberry dessert sauce

raspberries

Preheat oven to 350 degrees. To prepare crust, chop both nuts with a chef's knife to medium-fine. Place nuts on a jelly roll pan and toast in oven until light brown, about 7 minutes. Remove nuts from oven. Increase oven temperature to 400 degrees. Mix nuts with brown sugar and cinnamon; blend in melted butter. Cut piece of parchment paper to fit base of a 9-inch spring-form pan. Spray paper and sides of pan with non-stick cooking spray. With fingers, press crust mixture onto bottom of pan.

For filling, in a small bowl, combine sugar and cornstarch; set aside. With an electric mixer, in a large bowl, beat cream cheese and vanilla until smooth, about 5 minutes. With a rubber spatula, scrape down sides of bowl; add sugar mixture and beat on low speed 5 minutes. Add egg, yolks and cream. Pour into crust. Bake 45 minutes.

Meanwhile, for topping, combine sour cream, sugar and vanilla. Reduce oven temperature to 350 degrees; spread sour cream mixture over top to within ¼ inch of the edge. Bake 10 minutes. Cool thoroughly, then place in refrigerator overnight. Remove from pan.

TO PLATE: *Serve individual slice on a dessert plate. Garnish plate with raspberry dessert sauce and fresh raspberries.*

With a Fine Arts background from college and with several years of experience as an artist, Pastry Chef Carol Jordan applied for and received a two-year, state-certified apprenticeship at the Westin St. Francis Hotel in San Francisco. Afterwards, she spent ten years at the Sheraton Palace Hotel. She then returned to Alabama to the Grand Hotel, a 200-year old resort. More recently, she worked at the Beau Rivage Casino & Resort on the Mississippi Gulf Coast. Although she may have put her canvas and paints aside, the dessert plate now serves as her medium for creativity.

Trilogy: Almond Streusel Topped Apple Cobbler, Chocolate Mousse-Filled Box and "Butter" Cookie

YIELD: 6 TRILOGIES WHICH CAN BE SHARED

ALMOND STREUSEL TOPPED APPLE COBBLER

PREP TIME: 25 MINUTES PLUS 4 HOURS REFRIGERATION | COOK TIME: 50 MINUTES

EQUIPMENT NEEDED

6 (3½-inch) ramekins

1 box grater

APPLE COBBLER STREUSEL TOPPING

1¼ cups granulated sugar

½ cup margarine, cut into pieces, room temperature

½ cup vegetable shortening

2 ounces (¼ of an 8-ounce can) almond paste, crumbled

2 cups all purpose flour

1 teaspoon almond extract

APPLE COBBLER FILLING

2½ pounds (about 5) Golden Delicious apples, peeled, cored and ½-inch dice

2 tablespoons fresh lemon juice

⅓ cup packed light brown sugar

2 tablespoons granulated sugar

1½ tablespoons cornstarch

⅛ teaspoon ground nutmeg

¼ teaspoon cinnamon, plus sprinkle

¾ cup golden raisins

1 tablespoon brandy

½ teaspoon vanilla extract

For apple streusel topping, combine sugar, margarine, shortening and almond paste in a food processor; blend until smooth. Add flour and almond extract and mix just until combined. Form into a ball, wrap in plastic wrap and refrigerate about 4 hours or overnight.

Preheat oven to 350 degrees. Place 6 ramekins on a parchment-lined jelly roll pan. To make filling, in a bowl, combine apples with lemon juice. Add brown and granulated sugars, cornstarch, nutmeg, cinnamon, raisins, brandy and vanilla extract. Fill ramekin to top, packed with apple mixture. To top the apple filling, using the large holes on a box grater, hold ball of dough and grate the streusel topping all over the apple filling, forming a cone shape. Do not pack it down. Bake until golden brown, about 50 minutes.

This ultimate dessert is a combination of the creative masterpieces of three very talented chefs. The apple cobbler is a signature dessert of cookbook author, television celebrity, James Beard Award winning, Executive Chef Jeffrey Nathan of Abigael's. In the restaurant, this popular dish is served on its own and as part of a trilogy. The chocolate mousse-filled box is a signature dessert of Gitti Allman, pastry chef, who has studied under Colette Peters, Nick Malgieri, Toba Garrett and Roland Mesnier. She is the owner of Decorate My Cake on Long Island, New York. Finally, Hannah Frank, a home baker par excellence, is known far and wide for her baking delicacies. Guests flock to her, as they enthusiastically volunteer to sample anything from her kitchen. Most of all, they eagerly await the appearance of her famous butter cookies, which manage to disappear instantaneously.

(Continued on next page)

desserts

BROWNIES
PREP TIME: 10 MINUTES | COOK TIME: 30 MINUTES

- ⅓ cup granulated sugar
- ⅓ cup packed light brown sugar
- pinch of salt
- ½ cup all purpose flour
- 1 cup semi-sweet chocolate chips
- ¼ cup chocolate syrup
- ½ cup margarine
- 1 teaspoon vanilla extract
- 2 large eggs, lightly beaten

To make brownies, preheat oven to 350 degrees. Spray an 8-inch square baking pan with non-stick cooking spray. In a small bowl, stir granulated and brown sugars, salt and flour; set aside. Melt chocolate chips in a medium metal bowl set over a saucepan of simmering water. Cook over low heat, stirring continuously. Add syrup. Remove from heat. Add margarine and vanilla. Stir until smooth. Add 2 spoonfuls of chocolate mixture to beaten eggs, then pour egg mixture into chocolate. Stir until combined. Add dry ingredients to chocolate mixture. Blend thoroughly. Pour into prepared pan; bake 30 minutes. Cool completely in pan. Cut into 2-inch brownie squares.

MOUSSE
PREP TIME: 10 MINUTES | COOK TIME: 7 MINUTES

- ¾ cup semi-sweet chocolate chips
- 2 tablespoons canola oil
- 1¾ cups heavy cream or non-dairy whipping cream
- ¾ teaspoon rum

To prepare mousse, melt chocolate chips and oil together in the top of a double boiler or stainless steel bowl set over simmering water. Remove from heat and let stand until cool but still able to pour. Whip cream and rum with an electric mixer until stiff peaks form. Stir a spoonful of whipped cream into chocolate and then fold this mixture into the remaining cream until well combined. Cover with plastic and refrigerate.

CHOCOLATE BOX
PREP TIME: 20 MINUTES | COOK TIME: 7 MINUTES

- 2 cups semi-sweet chocolate chips

For chocolate box, with a ruler and a marker, draw a 12-inch square on a piece of wax paper. Turn paper face down on counter top. Over medium heat, melt chocolate chips in a bowl and set on top of a pot with simmering water. Stir chocolate until smooth. Cool slightly. With an offset spatula, spread melted chocolate onto wax paper, filling the marked square. When set, after 20 minutes, with a sharp knife (using a ruler), score into 2-inch squares. Peel away waxed paper. Place ¼ teaspoon of mousse on the bottom ¼ of the chocolate square. This acts as glue. Press "glue" of this chocolate square against 1 side of the brownie so that the chocolate square stands. This forms 1 side of the box. Repeat on other sides to construct the box. Chill for several hours until firm. Refrigerate boxes up to 24 hours. When ready to serve, spoon mousse into a pastry bag fitted with fluted tip. Pipe mousse into box.

MRS. FRANK'S "BUTTER" COOKIES

PREP TIME: 20 MINUTES | COOK TIME: 8-10 MINUTES

½ teaspoon ground cinnamon

3 tablespoons granulated sugar plus 1 cup minus 1 tablespoon, divided

2 sticks margarine

1 large egg

1½ teaspoons vanilla extract

2 cups plus 2 tablespoons all purpose flour, plus more if needed

¼ teaspoon salt

Preheat oven to 350 degrees. Combine cinnamon and 3 tablespoons sugar in a bowl. Set aside. With an electric mixer, cream together margarine and remaining sugar. Add egg, vanilla, flour and salt. If dough is sticky, add up to 6 tablespoons flour. Mix until combined. Line a cookie sheet with parchment paper or a reusable silicone mat. Remove dough from mixer and shape into small balls, placing them on cookie sheet with enough room in between to allow them to be flattened. Using a glass with a flat bottom, first press cookie dough balls down, then dip glass into sugar-cinnamon mixture. Finally, with cinnamon-coated glass, flatten dough until ⅛-inch thin. Bake 8-10 minutes. Remove cookies from pan onto a cooling rack. When cool, store in an airtight container.

GARNISH

1 (8-ounce) container non-dairy whipping cream, whipped

6 strawberries, halved

6 mint sprigs

6 small edible flowers (optional)

TO PLATE: *On a large plate, place warmed apple cobbler sprinkled with cinnamon, along with mousse-filled box, garnished with an edible flower and finally, a dollop of whipped cream, with cookie, 2 strawberry halves, and a sprig of mint.*

NOTE: *The only realistic way to prepare this dessert is to make the individual components in steps, reserving assembly for serving time. In a restaurant, a trilogy is typically a shared dessert. Any of these recipes can be served on their own.*

You will have leftover almond streusel topping; rewrap and freeze for later use.

There will be enough brownies left to serve on the side.

The cookies yield approximately 6 dozen and are great when you need a simple, delicious snack.

There are several ways to melt chocolate. Either place the chocolate in the top of a double boiler set over simmering water, or in a metal bowl fitted over a saucepan filled with an inch of simmering water (do not let the water touch the bowl), and stir until melted. Alternatively, microwave the chocolate in a glass bowl on medium power, in 30-second intervals, stirring in between, until chocolate is completely melted. If chocolate is being melted with butter, liqueur or some other liquid, it can be put into a saucepan directly over very low heat, stirring to avoid burning.

An offset spatula is a tool with a bent blade set in a short handle. The bent blade enables turning or lifting of foods from a pan that might otherwise be difficult to access. It is also very useful in the spreading of frosting or melted chocolate.

Chocolate Bobka

YIELD: 4 BOBKA LOAVES | PREP TIME: 20 MINUTES PLUS 2 HOURS RISING | COOK TIME: 30 MINUTES

DOUGH

- **7 cups all purpose flour plus 1 additional cup, if necessary**
- **6 (¼-ounce) packages or 4½ tablespoons instant yeast**
- **¾ cup granulated sugar**
- **1 tablespoon vanilla sugar, or 1 (.35 ounce) package**
- **1½ cups margarine, melted**
- **1¾ cups warm water**
- **2 large eggs**
- **2 yolks**
- **2 teaspoons salt**

CHOCOLATE FILLING

- **1 cup margarine, melted**
- **1 (4.1-ounce) box instant chocolate pudding**
- **1 large egg**
- **½ cup water**
- **2 cups granulated sugar**
- **1 cup cocoa**

CRUMB TOPPING

- **½ stick margarine**
- **1 cup all purpose flour**
- **¾ cup granulated sugar**

In a large bowl, combine flour, yeast, sugar, vanilla sugar, margarine, water, eggs, egg yolks and salt. Turn out on floured board and knead 5 minutes, adding up to 1 cup of flour if necessary. Allow to rise in a large bowl covered with plastic wrap for 1½ hours.

Meanwhile, prepare filling by combining margarine, chocolate pudding, egg, water, sugar and cocoa in a bowl. Set aside.

To make crumb topping, in a small bowl, crumble margarine with flour and sugar using fingertips.

Spray 4 (10-inch) loaf pans with non-stick cooking spray.

Divide dough into 8 pieces. Using a rolling pin, roll each piece into a ⅛-inch thick rectangle, the length of the loaf pan. Spread one-eighth of filling onto each rectangle, within 1 inch of the borders. Roll from long side like a jelly roll. Twist 2 rolls around each other and place a twist in each pan. Using all the crumbs, sprinkle one-fourth of crumbs on top of each bobka. Preheat oven to 350 degrees. Allow to rise 30 minutes, then bake 30 minutes. When cool enough to handle, remove from pans and allow to cool on a cooling rack. Slice when cool.

TO PLATE: *Serve sliced on a rectangular platter.*

NOTE: *Although this recipe uses a lot of margarine, notice that it does yield 4 bobkas. The bobkas freeze well when properly wrapped.*

Instant yeast, also called rapid-rise, is easy to use. It differs from active-dry yeast in that it does not need to be proofed (mixed with warm water and sugar resulting in a foamy liquid) and can be added directly to dry ingredients.

This recipe has been lovingly passed down from one generation to the next and is enjoyed every year at Cutler's Bungalow Colony. It is a delicious yeast cake that is a guaranteed treasure.

Peanut Butter Mousse Cake

SERVES: 12 | PREP TIME: 20 MINUTES PLUS MINIMUM 2 HOURS FOR CHILLING | COOK TIME: 15 MINUTES

CRUST

2 cups chocolate sandwich cookie crumbs

½ cup peanuts, chopped

¼ cup granulated sugar

2 tablespoons margarine, melted

MOUSSE

1¾ cups non-dairy whipping cream

2 cups creamy peanut butter

2 (8-ounce) containers tofutti cream cheese, room temperature

2 cups confectioners' sugar

2 tablespoons vanilla extract

TOPPING

¼ cup granulated sugar

¼ cup non-dairy whipping cream

1 cup semi-sweet chocolate chips

½ cup peanuts, chopped, for garnish

Preheat oven to 350 degrees. For crust, in a large bowl, combine cookie crumbs, peanuts, sugar and margarine. Press into a 10-inch springform pan. Bake 15 minutes. Set aside to cool.

For mousse, using an electric mixer, beat whipping cream until stiff. Set aside. In another mixing bowl, beat peanut butter and tofutti cream cheese together until smooth. Stir in confectioners' sugar and vanilla, mixing well. Gently fold in whipped cream, a quarter at a time. Pour into baked crust. Refrigerate until set, approximately 2 hours.

For topping, in a medium saucepan, combine sugar and whipping cream. Stir over medium heat until sugar dissolves and mixture comes to a boil. Remove from heat. Add chocolate chips and stir until melted and smooth. Remove cake from refrigerator. Spread topping evenly over filling. Garnish with peanuts. Refrigerate until cold, about 2 hours. Serve chilled.

TO PLATE: *Serve sliced on a dessert plate.*

NOTE: *To slice, remove cake from refrigerator. Dip a chef's knife into boiling water. Dry totally and then slice cake using a back and forth sawing motion so that chocolate topping does not crack.*

Netivot HaTorah's Day School's best selling cookbook, *Gatherings — Creative Kosher Cooking From Our Family To Yours* (2003), reflects the combined efforts of more than 130 dedicated parents. This outstanding non-dairy recipe is representative of that great cookbook.

Brownie Cookies

SERVES: 24 COOKIES | PREP TIME: 10 MINUTES PLUS 1 HOUR TO CHILL | COOK TIME: 14 MINUTES

½ cup all purpose flour
1 teaspoon baking powder
¼ teaspoon salt
¼ cup unsalted margarine or butter
3 ounces unsweetened chocolate, chopped
10 ounces bittersweet chocolate, chopped
1 teaspoon instant coffee
1 tablespoon hot water
½ teaspoon vanilla extract
4 large eggs
1⅓ cups granulated sugar
1 cup chocolate chips
1 cup chopped walnuts

Lightly spray two cookie sheets with non-stick cooking spray or line them with parchment paper. In small bowl, combine flour, baking powder and salt. Set aside. Melt margarine or butter with unsweetened and bittersweet chocolates in a microwavable bowl, checking every 15 seconds until melted. Set aside. In a separate small bowl, mix coffee, hot water and vanilla. Beat eggs, sugar and coffee mixture with an electric mixer on high for 6-8 minutes. Reduce speed and add melted chocolate. Continue to mix for 2 minutes. Reduce speed to low, add flour mixture and mix just until the ingredients are combined; over mixing the dough once the dry ingredients are added may result in tough cookies, or ones that do not rise. With a wooden spoon, stir in chocolate chips and walnuts. Refrigerate dough for 40 minutes. Use a ¼-cup measuring cup, a small ice cream scoop or a cookie scoop to place dough onto prepared cookie sheets, leaving 3 inches between the cookies. Put cookie sheets into the freezer for 20 minutes. It is important to note that in between batches, cookie dough should only be placed onto cooled cookie sheets. Transfer to preheated 350 degree oven and in batches, bake cookies until they are cracked on top but still appear moist, about 14 minutes. Do NOT over bake. Cool on cookie sheet pan until firm. Remove to wire racks and cool completely. Store in an airtight container.

TO PLATE: *Serve on a white plate accompanied by a big glass of milk.*

NOTE: *Having to refrigerate the dough and then freeze it is a bit time consuming. Rest assured that the finished product will prove to be very worthwhile. Chilling the dough before baking solidifies the fat and helps prevent overspreading as the cookies bake. Spooning a consistent amount of dough onto cookie sheets ensures even baking. Spray either the measuring cup or scoop with non-stick cooking spray to encourage easy release. Cooling racks allow air to circulate under the cookies so that they do not become soggy.*

The first time I witnessed the power of these over-the-top chocolate cookies, was while taking a course in food styling at the Culinary Institute of America. There is a very busy coffee shop that attracts tourists coming to visit the school. The line for these irresistible treats is literally out the door and around the corridor. The cookies cry for a big glass of milk to accompany them, so kick back and enjoy! This recipe has been adapted from *Baking Boot Camp* (John Wiley & Sons 2007).

Moist Orange-Pineapple Bundt Cake

YIELD: 1 (12-CUP) BUNDT CAKE | PREP TIME: 10 MINUTES | COOK TIME: 1 HOUR

CAKE

1½ cups canola oil

4 large eggs

2 cups granulated sugar

1 teaspoon vanilla extract

½ cup orange juice

1 (6-ounce) can pineapple juice

1 teaspoon grated orange zest

3 cups all purpose flour

1 tablespoon baking powder

½ teaspoon salt

OPTIONAL ORANGE STRIP GARNISH

1 orange peel

¼ cup granulated sugar

½ cup water

OPTIONAL GLAZE

1 cup confectioners' sugar

1½ tablespoons orange juice

Often the best recipes come right from the kitchens of amazing bakers. This recipe is great to have amongst your repertoire. Serve with or without the glaze and garnish.

Preheat oven to 350 degrees. Spray a Bundt pan with non-stick cooking spray. In the bowl of a food processor, mix oil, eggs and sugar. Add vanilla, orange and pineapple juices, and orange zest. In a separate bowl, combine flour, baking powder and salt. Add flour mixture to food processor bowl and pulse until combined, but avoid over-mixing. Pour into prepared pan; bake 1 hour.

While cake is baking, prepare orange strip garnish. Using a grooved citrus zester, cut a strip of peel from around the orange until there are several long strips. Put sugar and water in a pot. Add peel; simmer until tender, about 5 minutes. Remove strips from liquid and allow to cool on parchment paper. Set aside. When cake is done, cool 10 minutes, then invert onto a rack set over a tray and cool cake completely.

For glaze, in a small bowl, with wire whisk, combine confectioners' sugar and orange juice. Pour over cake, allowing glaze to drizzle down sides.

TO PLATE: *Serve individually sliced with orange strip for garnish.*

NOTE: *For orange peel garnish, if you do not have a zester, use a peeler to remove zest. Trim zest into a rectangle, then with a chef's knife, cut into thin strips, approximately the size of matchsticks (also known as julienne).*

If using a dark, non-stick baking pan, count on shorter baking time or reduce baking temperature by 25 degrees.

Sugar, aside from its capacity to sweeten, is also used in the culinary kitchen to accelerate the browning of meats and vegetables. In the pastry kitchen it tenderizes dough, provides texture, and gives stability to egg whites whipped into meringues. Granulated sugar or table sugar is the most versatile. Brown sugar, whether light or dark, is white sugar with molasses added. Confectioners' (powdered) sugar is ground to a fine powder and mixed with a small amount of cornstarch. It is used for icings because it dissolves easily and is also used as a decorative dusting on baked goods.

Mango Feuillantine

SERVES: 8-9 | PREP TIME: 35 MINUTES | COOK TIME: 1 HOUR

PASTRY PINWHEELS

½ (17.3-ounce) package puff pastry sheets (1 sheet), room temperature

1 large egg, lightly beaten

Preheat oven to 350 degrees. Line a jelly roll pan with parchment paper. Place 1 sheet of puff pastry onto jelly roll pan. Cut puff pastry into 9 individual squares. For each square, use a paring knife to cut from each corner towards center, stopping 1 inch from center. You will have a 1-inch circle in the center of each square and all of the corners will be cut in half. Lift every other point, folding it towards center of circle, gently pressing points to meet, forming a pinwheel. Brush with beaten egg; bake until golden brown, about 20 minutes.

PASTRY CREAM

2 egg yolks

3 tablespoons granulated sugar

1 tablespoon all purpose flour

½ cup soy or non-dairy milk, chilled

¼ teaspoon vanilla extract

Prepare pastry cream by bringing water to a boil in the bottom of a double boiler; let simmer. Put egg yolks into a bowl. Add sugar and flour. Stir with a wooden spoon until yolks turn light yellow color. Slowly add soy milk. Place bowl on top of double boiler. Add vanilla. Stir constantly until mixture is thick and coats back of spoon. Do not allow cream to boil. Once thickened, after about 15 minutes, remove from hot water and continue stirring 2-3 minutes. Place plastic wrap directly on top of pastry cream and refrigerate.

MANGO

1 cup granulated sugar

2 tablespoons margarine

2 mangoes, peeled, pitted, sliced in wedges

2 cinnamon sticks

To prepare mangoes, heat sugar with margarine in a saucepan over medium heat until sugar dissolves, about 5 minutes. When light brown, add mangoes and cinnamon sticks. Simmer on low heat 20 minutes. Remove and discard cinnamon sticks.

MANGO AND STRAWBERRY PURÉE

1 ripe mango

1 cup granulated sugar, divided

2 tablespoons corn syrup, divided

½ (20-ounce) package frozen strawberries

For mango purée, add mango, ½ cup sugar and 1 tablespoon corn syrup to blender. Purée until smooth. Repeat same method for strawberry purée, using frozen strawberries and remaining sugar and corn syrup.

ITALIAN MERINGUE
- ½ cup granulated sugar
- 2 tablespoons water
- 2 egg whites

For meringue, combine sugar and water in a small pot. Boil until sugar is dissolved. Cover pan, lower heat and simmer. Beat whites with an electric mixer. When stiff, turn heat up until sugar syrup bubbles slightly. Remove from heat. With mixer running slowly, pour sugar syrup in thin stream into egg whites. Beat until meringue is shiny. This whole process should take about 15 minutes. Fold meringue into pastry cream.

GARNISH
- confectioners' sugar

To assemble, preheat oven to 325 degrees. Slice pinwheel pastry in half, with a serrated bread knife, like a sandwich roll. On bottom half, spoon on some cream and mango slices. Cover with top pastry lid. Bake 2-3 minutes, just to warm. Sprinkle with confectioners' sugar.

TO PLATE: *Ladle or spoon 3 tablespoons mango purée into the center of a dessert plate, smoothing it into an even layer with back of ladle. Using squeeze bottle and working from center of plate toward edge, make a spiral of strawberry purée. Starting at center of plate, pull tip of wooden skewer through sauces to make web effect. Place pastry in center.*

NOTE: *This recipe is time consuming! However, each of the components can be prepared in advance, allowing for easy assembly prior to serving. The finished result is spectacular!*

An Italian meringue, made by whipping hot sugar syrup into beaten egg whites, is incredibly versatile and more stable than a regular meringue. One of the keys to successfully beating egg whites is to separate the eggs straight from the refrigerator then wait for them to reach room temperature before beating them.

When using a fruit purée, dessert fruit syrup or even a chocolate syrup, there are at least 6 different techniques that can be employed to decorate the plate. Here we have used a spider web effect. To create hearts, place three pools of mango purée along the side of the plate. Squeeze a dime size of strawberry purée into the center of each mango pool. Draw the tip of a wooden skewer in a continuous motion through all of the pools to form three consecutive hearts. To create bars, spoon the mango purée into the center of the plate. With the back of a ladle, smooth purée in an even layer. With a squeeze bottle of strawberry purée, create a sequence of parallel lines across the plate. Using the tip of a wooden skewer draw several perpendicular lines through the parallel lines. To make an informal presentation, using a squeeze bottle, place random size dots around plate. You can use one or both of the sauces. Simple casual striping is accomplished by squeezing the bottle of purée with even pressure back and forth across the dessert. Finally, a serpentine can be made by squeezing the purée around the outside perimeter of the plate in the shape of a backwards "S." Begin the second "S" just above the bottom of the first so that they look as though they are interlocking. Continue the pattern around the plate. To finish, place dots around the outer edge of the serpentine to complete the effect.

New York's La Carne Grill was most fortunate when they hired Chef Cheikh Samba, originally from Senegal, West Africa, with on-the-job training from the Meridian Hotel. His desserts are masterpieces, not only in appearance, but taste as well, a feat when preparing non-dairy desserts in a meat kitchen.

index

index

index

index

index

index

index

index